AF481126

The POWER of LOVING, FORGIVING & FORGETTING

If You Are Loving Enough, Forgiving Enough, and Forgetting Enough, You Become the Happiest Person in The Universe.

FRANK A. DE LA ROSA

Au
Authorunit
Printing your dreams

CONTENTS

AUTHOR: Frank A. De La Rosa
TITLE: The Power of Loving, Forgiving, Forgetting
ISBN: 979-8-89030-153-6 (Paperback Edition)
ISBN: 979-8-89030-154-3 (E-book Edition)
Pages: 144
Reviewed by: Nicole Miller

Royal Book Review

Frank A. De La Rosa's "The Power of Loving, Forgiving & Forgetting" is an emotionally resonant narrative that follows the journey of a Filipino protagonist, navigating a series of formidable challenges and ultimately discovering hope in a foreign land. De La Rosa's compassionate narrative voice and astute storytelling delve deep into the complexities of life's tribulations and illuminate the path toward triumph.

What sets De La Rosa's work apart is his exceptional talent for painting vivid scenes that shaped his life. His descriptive prowess renders his story relatable and forges an intimate connection between the reader and the subject matter.

As I immersed myself in De La Rosa's prose, I was struck by how deftly he etched the contours of his experiences. His words provide a crystal-clear and intricate portrayal, forging a potent emotional tie between reader and material, rendering it an extraordinarily compelling and immersive read.

Daisy, a central figure in the narrative, transcends the confines of a conventional wife. She embodies the spirit of a true warrior, bravely confronting life's challenges. Daisy's unyielding faith and relentless determination shine through her battle against cancer, a struggle she faced hand in hand with her husband, Frank. Their journey through adversity is an inspiration of unwavering resilience and a beacon of hope. It stands as a testament that, armed with faith in a higher power, we possess the strength to overcome any obstacle in our path.

De La Rosa's unparalleled storytelling skills are evident in how he masterfully weaves complex themes of sacrifice, love, family, and faith to create a captivating and thought-provoking narrative. His writing style is characterized by fluidity and elegance, enabling him to effortlessly convey the most intricate emotions. The author's deft treatment of these themes imbues his work with a timeless quality that resonates with readers, leaving an indelible mark on their hearts and minds. Long after the final page is turned, his story stirs a deep contemplation that lingers within the reader's soul.

As I delved into Frank A. De La Rosa's "The Power of Loving, Forgiving & Forgetting," I was struck by the depth of its message. This book speaks to the core of our being, highlighting the overwhelming importance of love, forgiveness, and the ability to let go. The author's words served as a beacon of hope, reminding me that by embodying these values, we can find inner peace and claim our place among the happiest souls in the universe. The book's profound insights and moving narratives left me feeling uplifted, and I would recommend it to anyone seeking to understand the power of love and forgiveness better.

The Power of Loving, Forgiving & Forgetting
Author: Frank A. De La Rosa
Title: The Power of Loving, Forgiving & Forgetting
ISBN: 979-8-89030-153-6 (Paperback Edition)
ISBN: 979-8-89030-154-3 (E-book Edition)
Pages: 144
Reviewed by: Samantha Jones

Book Review

Potential Cinematic Gem: A Call to Filmmakers

Frank A. De La Rosa's outstanding book, "The Power of Loving, Forgiving & Forgetting," is a captivating masterpiece that is sure to leave readers spellbound. This exceptional work of literature has all the makings of a cinematic masterpiece, with its emotionally resonant story and complex and well-developed characters. It has the power to stir deep-seated emotions in its readers and leave them pondering on the universal themes of love, forgiveness, and redemption.

This story follows a Filipino protagonist's journey in a foreign land, facing many difficult challenges. However, through this journey, the protagonist discovers hope, making it a tale that can touch the hearts of audiences worldwide. De La Rosa's vivid depiction of his life, including his recovery from the aftermath of World War II and poverty, provides a strong foundation for a film that promises both entertainment and meaningful contemplation. The emotional trajectory of the story is potent and has the potential to leave a lasting impression on viewers. Within this narrative, the characters are ripe for cinematic exploration, bringing their complexities to life.

Moreover, the book explores a complex and intriguing theme that allows for creative imagination and captivating visual storytelling. It tells the story of Frank, who overcomes seemingly insurmountable challenges such as the loss of his wife, the closure of his store, and confrontations with his family. The story's emotional impact, combined with the potential for stunning visuals, has the power to captivate and leave a profound impression on its readers.

De La Rosa's writing style is a masterful blend of rich language and vivid imagery, perfectly suited for bringing stories to life on the big screen. His ability to craft compelling descriptions and evoke powerful emotions through words makes his work a treasure trove of visual potential. Any skilled director who takes on the challenge of adapting De La Rosa's writing will find themselves with a wealth of material to work with, capable of creating a film that seamlessly captures the beauty and depth of the original text. With careful pacing and expert direction, the result would be a truly unforgettable cinematic experience.

"The Power of Loving, Forgiving & Forgetting" is an awe-inspiring and heartwarming book that has the potential to capture the imaginations of movie lovers. The characters in the book are not only relatable but also inspiring, and their stories are bound to leave a lasting impact on the readers. Filmmakers looking to create a powerful and unforgettable story should definitely consider taking inspiration from this book.

Dedication

$\mathcal{I}$ would like to dedicate this book to my former high school instructor and mentor, Mr. Eliseo R. Cabangon, of CAIC in Catanduanes, Philippines. His teachings in English Exploratory Writing and English Literature greatly inspired me and contributed to my success as a Literary Writer in the United States of America. I owe him a great deal for providing me with the knowledge and wisdom that has guided me throughout my life. Mr. Cabangon will always hold a special place in my heart as my former instructor and mentor during my formative years in high school. May he rest in peace and be forever remembered, with the perpetual light of heaven shining upon him.

About the Author

*F*rank A. De La Rosa, like numerous resilient Filipinos who have overcome adversity, embarked on a personal quest for a brighter future beyond his homeland. As a young man, he recognized that he needed to persevere for him and his family.

Frank wholeheartedly acknowledges that he is never alone in his remarkable journey. With God as his guiding force, he remains grounded and motivated. Through their unwavering connection and Frank's unfaltering dedication, he has transformed his humble beginnings, victories, and tribulations into seven captivating books: "A Touch of Life," "The Thing of Beauty is a Joy Forever," "Pan American Flight #863 to Paradise" (in three volumes), "Frank's Magical Farm" and "Beyond Forgetting."

You can find these books on Amazon, and they are also prominently featured on Frank's official webpage, www.frankadelarosa.com.

Acknowledgements

$\mathcal{A}$s I work on completing my eighth book, "Loving Enough, Forgiving Enough, & Forgetting Enough," I am considering who to acknowledge for their contributions. After much thought, I have narrowed down the list. This book has been the most challenging one for me to write, and I believe it requires a skilled journalist to do its justice. However, having written seven previous books, I have come to realize that I am an accomplished writer myself. This book is powerful, compelling, and poignant in its own way. Without further ado, I would like to acknowledge the following individuals who have supported me throughout this journey:

I received a call from **Tomas Curtis**, my literary agent at Author Unit Publishing Company, after ten years of publishing my first book, A Touch of Life. Tom was a young and enthusiastic man with high ambitions. I had been on a sabbatical due to some family deaths when he called me unexpectedly during Christmas of 2020. Our conversation did not end there, and Tom kept calling me for days, weeks, and months. Eventually, he convinced me to republish my book as a second edition with a 25-35% lower price. I was swayed by his sweet and persuasive words, and we both had many dreams for my book. The second edition went viral after publishing, and people from all over responded. When Tom informed me of the number of people who reacted to my book, I was ecstatic and overjoyed, feeling like I was on cloud #9!

I have a sister-in-law named **Maria Cleofe Garcia Melchor** who resides in the Philippines. She works as a Financial Consultant for an Investment Company located in Manila's Military Installations. Maria is a trusted family connection with whom I confide in and seek advice from. She possesses a wealth of knowledge and wisdom that she willingly shares with me. Her encouragement has motivated me to continue writing more books. Maria even believes that I have the potential to become a movie mogul someday. I am working hard to make my dreams come true, and with the help of God, anything is possible. I hold my dreams close to my heart, and Maria has been instrumental in my success with my published books, A Touch of Life and Beyond Forgetting.

I received a Book Review of my First Book, A Touch of Life, second edition, from **Ms. Judee V. Mendoza**, a Professional Teacher in the Philippines. Her review was profound, powerful, and compelling, and it touched me to the core. Ms. Mendoza's encouragement has been a driving force behind my desire to write more good books. I view my readers and book reviewers as my inspiration, and Ms. Mendoza certainly played a significant role in my writing adventure. I cannot thank her enough for being a part of my books and the successes they have garnered.

Dear **Readers** and **Facebook friends**, I'd like to take a moment to express my gratitude for your kind words, supportive comments, and appreciation for the wisdom and knowledge I share. Your presence and encouragement have played an important role in my success, and I feel truly blessed to have you as a part of my journey. Thank you for your continued support and for taking the time to engage with my content. I look forward to sharing more with you in the future.

CHAPTER I

· · · · ·

School Days

During my first and second years at university, I enrolled in general education courses, Educational Psychology, College Algebra, Logic, Freshman English, Spanish I, II, III, & IV, General Chemistry, Inorganic Chemistry, Animal Husbandry, College Physics, to name a few.

I commuted to school every day from Cubao, Quezon City, where I resided, to Caloocan by bus, then hopped in a jeepney to continue my trip to the Araneta University campus. One way, it was a ten-kilometer trip. Although it was a long ride, made much longer, often due to snarls and stalls in traffic, it was a lot of fun. Many of my fellow students took the same route every day, and the trip's monotony was relieved by a lot of chatter among us about goings on the campus, comparing notes and lectures, and updates on a more social and personal level. Living in a tropical climate could pose challenges in commuting, though, especially during the rainy season. This was when it became exceedingly difficult to commute because I and the rest of the commuters had to battle not only rain, gusty wind, and swirling flood. I also had to endure

horrible traffic, wet clothes, muddy feet, and runny noses. At times like these, I usually came home after dark, tired, wet, and hungry, but thanking the Lord that I made it home sound of body and mind. It was challenging when one lived a long distance from the school. However, bad weather and traffic were only some of life's roadblocks that we must face daily and overcome as we go on about our daily lives.

As a sidebar, I mentioned earlier that I used to ride jeepneys while traveling to and from school. Jeepneys as a means of public transportation are, I found out later, unique to the Philippines. I'm proud to say they are a product of Filipino creativity and ingenuity. Originally called jitneys, they were surplus vehicles left by the Americans by the thousands after the war. Our enterprising fellow citizens saw an opportunity to make cars a means of mass transportation. They began refurbishing these vehicles to make them passenger and road worthy. Soon, jeepneys were a common sight on the streets and were called "kings of the road" because of their enormous size and capacity to sit more than double the passengers a jitney could accommodate. The body of the jeepney was typically painted in festive colors and usually trimmed with shiny chrome. Painted inside the jeepney and on the partition between the driver's seat and the passengers' section were expressions that are typical of Filipino wit, like "barya lang po sa umaga," which means "please pay in loose change in the morning" because the driver has not yet earned enough to change bills; or "Hudas did not pay," "Hudas" refers to Judas Iscariot who betrayed Jesus Christ, hence one betrays a trust if one does not pay his fare; or "upong singko lang po" is an appeal to sit straight and not slouch so as not to take up space intended for other passengers to sit. Owners and drivers decorated their vehicles so that they attract more would-be passengers. They would put religious icons or statues on their dashboards and hang ribbons or banners with prayers invoking God's protection while on the road. Others would hang flags, plastic flowers, and other colorful trinkets and lights that made their vehicle look very festive. Add to the whole mix music emanating from speakers, and the jeepney was a spectacle to behold, like a fiesta on the go!

I enrolled in the regular program in Agricultural Engineering consisting of ten (10) semesters but did not attend summer classes. Instead, I spent summers gardening for my neighbors back home in Cubao. Not only did I mow lawns, cut grass, pull up weeds or clean up rubbish in the yards for my more affluent clients, but I also potted or repotted flowers and herbs, dug and prepared flower and vegetable beds, planted seeds and cuttings, made borders and hedges using shrubs under the direction of my clients and aided by my advice on what greenery is best suited. I also ensured all the plants and animals under my temporary care were amply watered and fed. It was an opportunity I did not pass on as it gave me a chance not only to apply my burgeoning knowledge in my chosen field of study, Agriculture, and those that I learned from my father when I was just a young boy, but it also enabled me to earn an income to help augment my school expenses and daily allowance. It was hard and dirty work throughout the long and fiercely hot summer. I had already learned so much about farming and the care of farm animals from my father as I helped him around his farm while I was growing up, and I found this knowledge very useful during this time. I was drenched in sweat by midday, and my muscles were protesting by the day's end. But earning a chunk of cash was a good incentive, and working on my strengths daily gave me an excellent physique.

As children, my siblings and I were taught to be respectful of everybody regardless of their age or station in life. This upbringing and being cheerful by nature made me the recipient of the goodwill of our neighbors and the people I worked for. They showed appreciation by giving me cool drinks and snacks during my breaks and food to take home. All in all, summers were an enjoyable and profitable experience for me. For relaxation, I and my siblings would play games together or sit together and chat and crack jokes after lunch or dinner. As a teenager, I would have loved going on picnics and dances, but as a poor student, sacrifices had to be made. I knew that at this time, I had to forgo many of the pleasures a teenage person would enjoy being able to continue my studies and finish my course. Sacrifices had to be endured, and a strict budget should be followed. Study hard, sacrifice a lot, and pray with all my heart for inspiration and endurance. I was focused on my goals and would give my all to succeed.

All in all, I must finish ten semesters of college to earn my degree in Agricultural Engineering. I considered that time, ten semesters, an excellent investment for my professional future. Whatever I do must affect my family's well-being, too, so I knew I must take full advantage of the blessing, in the form of a full scholarship, that I was enjoying. I look around me and see that we all are students preparing for a promising future. For many students and their families, earning a degree was their only hope to emerge from the dark despair of poverty. Many of them were in the same financially strapped boat as I was; many were in a lot worse state. I was fortunate in being a recipient of a full scholarship. I did not have to be a working student like some of my schoolmates, who had to juggle studies and schoolwork simultaneously. Inevitably one or the other suffered. One's health or schoolwork suffered. I realized then that hardship is an integral part of life and that since I decided to go on and pursue my dream of finishing my studies, I should keep on going and never give up my grasp on life. Sometimes, with God's grace, people receive blessings in one form or another to help alleviate their burdens. Still, in the end, it is their decision that leads them to continue the journey they must undertake that would lead them to realize our goals.

I was a very active student on the college campus and joined clubs and organizations that attracted my interest. I was a member of the Araneta University Honor Society and was voted into the office of Vice President. I was also a Philippine Agricultural Engineers Society member and was elected Treasurer. I joined the National Union of Students and was voted Secretary of the Department of Engineering; I was also a departmental editor of The Harvest Yearbook 1963. I was a College Reserve Officers Training Corps member from 1958 to 1960.

For me, the final three years of college were hectic and physically and mentally draining. I had to juggle time to accommodate everything on my schedule. I had to hurdle all the science courses listed in my curriculum. I spent long nights studying, analyzing, and solving problems in different fields of Mathematics, like Geometry, Analytic Geometry, Descriptive Geometry, Trigonometry, Differential Calculus, Integral Calculus, Differential Equations, Physics, Hydraulics, Thermodynamics & Surveying. Through it all,

I endured by thinking of the sacrifices my parents were making for me and my siblings, their hopes and expectations, and my dream of earning a college diploma to give myself a chance for a better life. My family's words of encouragement were a constant inspiration to me, and they assured me that they would always be a rock I could depend on. They asked me to keep faith in them and my faith in God strong through constant prayers, but most of all, I must believe in myself and my abilities and that this confidence in myself would take me to the realization of my goals.

If long nights were spent by me in constant study, writing reports, or doing projects, so were my waking hours. Added to that was the myriad of extra-curricular activities I had to attend to and obligations to various organizations to fulfill being an active member and or officer, as the case may be. I had to participate in meetings and go on course-related field trips, collect samples of soil, plants, and wood, observe the care and progress of animals on farms, and inspect plants and trees growing in lowlands, in highlands, in wet or dry climates, identify the natural habitats of particular plant and animal specimen, survey areas, identify boundaries and draw diagrams and maps, write tons of reports on those various observations and inspections, spend time in the library doing research and meet up with my study groups. Sometimes I had to be present at social gatherings, being a scholar of the university and officer of various organizations to keep my social network active and current, to take a break from thinking of things academically, and savor the presence of and conversation with friends, fellow students, and mentors. I would often have to skip meals because I had to hurry to have papers typed, printed, or bound or rush to meet the deadline for submitting projects.

Truthfully, summers were the only times that I ate regular meals and slept more than three to four hours a night. My mother used to prepare simple meals which the whole family partook of and enjoyed together, not hurrying through the meals but enjoying the time of togetherness and telling each other about our day. Hearty meals and a full day of physical labor made me sleep like a log at night. At school, I had to make do with a cup of coffee, drinking on the run as my breakfast, and just a wink or two of sleep at night. Add to that, I had to find time to attend to my laundry, personal grooming, and other mundane things. It was usual to ask myself if I had time to poop, bathe, brush my teeth, cut my nails, shave, go to the barbershop for a haircut, iron my clothes, and shine my shoes? I told myself I did not have time to go a-courting or see a movie, which I could not afford anyway, or hang out with friends and chat, watch basketball, and cheer for our favorite teams. Relaxation or recreation took a lot of work to come by with a schedule as full as mine. As always, I would tell myself to carry on with God's grace.

It was a real roller coaster ride of college life for me. But at last, with God on my side, I could tackle all my schoolwork and many extra-curricular loads on the side and have relieved and grateful sighs. I thanked my alma mater, my dear professors, and my mentors for helping me fulfill my dream of earning a college degree, for without them all, I could not be what I am today. To God Be the Glory Forever.

Looking back as I marched across that big stage at the Araneta University Auditorium, wearing my cap and gown, I could not describe my feeling of ecstasy after overcoming the hurdles, the sacrifices, the endless nights of study, the dizzying rush through the days of classes and lectures, research, the frenzy of writing and rewriting notes, essays, project studies, and theses, drawing diagrams and sketching maps, praying all the while that everything would be typed, printed and bound and submitted on or before the deadline.

My mantra of carrying on and never giving up enabled me to graduate from high school as class valedictorian and earn a degree in college with Latin honors, *Cum Laude.* I was determined to adopt the same attitude to secure a postgraduate scholarship at one of the universities abroad. I was particular that there was always a reward waiting for someone like me who does well in school, and I felt so blessed knowing that God was with me all the time.

On my graduation day, March 23, 1963, my dear father, a humble farmer by profession, was there to join and celebrate with me, the family's first college graduate. Along with four of my siblings and some close relatives, they traveled five hundred miles from our home province to join me on my graduation day. They were all as overjoyed as I was to be with them on my graduation day. When the last graduate had gone down onto the stage, the mass group of graduates gave a loud whoop and threw their mortarboards up in the air. My family prayed and gave wholehearted thanks to God and my mentors, who congratulated me for my dedication to my studies.

· · · · ·

CHAPTER II

After Graduation

My diploma and college transcripts were my passports to the professional world. Without these credentials, which were incontestably stellar, I believed I would never be offered a job or a position because of the hundreds of thousands of new graduates every year. Studying hard, working hard, self-determination, sacrifices, perseverance, and faith in God, all together, was my sure-fire recipe for success.

After graduation, we, the new graduates, were now on our own, all with our ears to the ground for any rumors or information about vacancies and job opportunities in our preferred fields of study. If those were not available, anything to gain experience would do. Hopeful and very eager, with so many questions in our minds, we were all out in the world seeking any possibility of getting hired. With hundreds of thousands of new graduates each year, we knew there needed to be more jobs for everyone. That was a big challenge for us. In man's need to provide for himself and their families better lives, they always seek greener pastures. Who can blame those professionals who cannot land jobs in their chosen careers if they decide to settle for positions currently available to them? After all, if a person cannot afford to pass up an opportunity to earn an honest living while waiting for options better suited to their degrees, they should grab the available ones. It is a fact that many professionals are forced to settle for less-than-suitable jobs. Hunger pangs cannot be rescheduled or postponed; people must eat, pay bills, and purchase other necessities to make it from one day to the next. It is no surprise that thousands of our fellow citizens seek employment abroad. If they are lucky and meet the requirements and standards of their desired positions, they get to work in careers suitable to their training. Otherwise, they must return to school to earn credits to fulfill those requirements. While earning those credits, however, they have to endure and make do with lesser-paying jobs where they can find them to survive within this period. They generally waited on tables, pumped gas, drove taxis, and served as cashiers, bellhops, concierges, and janitors, jobs they wouldn't do if they were in their own country.

During my graduation, our country did not suffer as severe a drain in the workforce as it did in later years. When the peso's value continued to decline compared to the dollar, more and more job seekers were enticed to seek employment abroad. As inflation worsened, so did the country's unemployment percentage. More and more people sought employment abroad. Filipinos who worked abroad were called Overseas Filipino Workers or OFWs. The government later had to establish an office in the Philippines and in embassies in different countries dedicated to taking care of and overseeing their needs and addressing their concerns. And who would have guessed that this exodus of the workforce would hugely benefit our country through vast dollar remittances sent by overseas workers to their families every month? These remittances constituted a large percentage of the country's annual dollar earnings. The massive exodus of professionals looking for greener pastures in various countries would later be called the "brain drain." Filipino workers were soon scattered around the world on job-hunting quests and were much in demand when they were found to be professional in the manner in the workplace, diligent, patient, conscientious, and creative. Their bosses greatly appreciated them, and there was a clamor for more Filipino workers. (Of course, the plight of domestic workers is a different sad story that will not be discussed here, although their dollar remittances are just as helpful revenue.) Much sooner than expected, I would be given an opportunity to join the ranks of this departure.

I consider myself to be one of the lucky graduates of 1963. I had been informed of a job opportunity at the Bureau of Soils and was urged to call and set an appointment for an interview. I was told to come at a particular time and date and bring my diploma, transcript, and personal data. Although I felt very nervous and apprehensive, it was my first application for a job. I was looking forward to my interview at the Bureau of Soils. As it happened, my apprehension was baseless because the discussion went on so well. I had to see Mr. Solis, the manager of the Bureau of Soils.

There were several applicants waiting in the outer office who were individually ushered into Mr. Solis' office by his secretary. When my turn came, I steeled myself and went inside to meet Mr. Solis. The secretary introduced me and Mr. Solis to each other. The manager's friendly and calm manner put me at ease. I took out my papers and diploma from my portfolio, and as I handed them to Mr. Solis for perusal, I looked at him eye to eye. After reading my writings, he asked me when I would be available to start work. And just like that, I had landed a job! I was no longer a statistic in the column of the unemployed. Mr. Solis told me that it was mine if I wanted the Soil Engineer job. I stuttered in amazement and answered humbly and softly that I was ready whenever needed. I thanked Mr. Solis profusely and told him I was prepared to report for duty at any time. Immediately I offered a prayer in my mind thanking God for this timely blessing and for helping me keep my spirits up through all my years in college. My belief that hard work is its own reward was strengthened. I also prayed that many graduates would be as lucky as I had landed a job at the first opportunity.

I did not start on the job right away after being hired. I had to undergo briefing and attend training seminars together with those newly hired, like me, in preparation for our respective duties and responsibilities. It was back to the classroom for me and my fellow trainees. So, for a period of one month, I listened attentively to more scientific lectures, learned protocols, and watched demonstrations on how things were supposed to be done and run. At the end of the month, all trainees were asked to write an essay about our experiences at the Central Office. After the end of the period, we were asked to submit our respective articles. Mr. Francis, who oversaw the training program, collected all the essays. He immediately began to read all the papers that the trainees submitted. Finally, he made an announcement, loud and clear, that the best essay for this training period was presented by Francisco A. De La Rosa, from Araneta University. It was another very proud moment for me, and I could not believe I was judged to have submitted the best essay. Five years of writing reports in college gave me excellent training in writing.

For that year, our group of trainees was considered the cream of the crop of agriculture graduates from different colleges and universities all over the country, and I was at the top!

I was destined to enjoy a surfeit of good news, and why not? One cannot have too much of it. After we were released from the Central Office in Manila, good news awaited me in my Cubao, Quezon City residence. The excellent information consisted of two parts. First, I was admitted to the Graduate School of the University of California, Davis, in California, United States, and second, at the same time, I was offered a job as a Graduate Research Assistant at the Department of Agricultural Engineering at the same institution. The University of California, Davis (or UC Davis, as it is usually called) is a learning institution in Northern California in the City of Davis. It is one of several University of California campuses and is considered a public Ivy League school. It is famous for its outstanding programs in biological and agricultural sciences.

For this reason, it is considered the top training school for agricultural engineers in the United States. God is truly perfect in His timing! Just a few hours before I was to begin my career as a Soil Engineer, I received this good news from the University of California, Davis. I did not regret not being able to continue my job as a Soil Engineer as I was given a much better offer. I became very excited to prepare for my trip to the United States of America.

CHAPTER III

• • • • •

The Preparation for the Trip to The United States of America

My circle, consisting of schoolmates and mentors in school and my friends, was unaware of my impending preparations for my sojourn to the United States of America. I didn't update anyone on my plans except for my family. Although the job in California was a sure-fire thing, I still inexplicably harbored doubts in my mind. What if I announced the good news to my circle of friends and mentors, and for some reason, things do not push through in the end? I knew I could not bear the disappointment, embarrassment, and humiliation of it all. When suffering doubt and indecision, I did what I had always done before; I prayed to God for guidance and enlightenment. In the end, I decided to inform everybody and share my good news so that they could also be happy for me, and they were because they believed I was destined for bigger things. I was at a crossroads at this point in my life, and I would be crossing an ocean (or flying over it) to live the life that fate had already set for me. I immediately communicated with the University of California, Davis, and conveyed my acceptance of both offers. I again prayed to God that my preparations would go smoothly and not be hindered by unexpected setbacks or complications. The suggestion given to me was unique and delivered only to a select few. Not taking advantage of the opportunity to study and work in a premier university would be a sacrilege.

My family was sad that I was about to leave them, but their sadness was tempered by the good fortune that befell me. I was also sorry to have to leave my family. I would miss the growing-up years of my younger siblings. I wanted to be there with them and be their big brother as they became young men and women. The years of building a strong sibling bond between brothers and sisters may take time and effort. They need to have shared experiences at play and in familial activities to share that undeniable feeling of belonging, trust, and love that only family members have for each other forged through the years. They can be each other's rock in times of tribulation, knowing that each of them has each other's back, will not be judged, and belong to this family that accepts them and loves them unconditionally. I promised to help them in every way I could, even if a large ocean lay between us, distance did not matter, for they were my family, and I loved them.

CHAPTER IV

· · · · ·

Getting Documents

I had heard many horror stories about obtaining the necessary papers needed to travel abroad, and I had a lot of documents that needed processing. I had heard talk of corrupt practices indulged in by employees in government offices wherein these papers were to be processed. I heard of rumors that employees usually ignore or delay the processing of documents if their palms are not greased enough with cash or that clients would be given the runaround. Clients would be told that their papers have yet to reach this desk, so perhaps it was still being processed at a particular desk on a specific floor, above or below the office. The poor clients following up on their papers would be huffing and puffing up or down the stairs wherever they were directed.

Due to my impending travel abroad, I had to apply for a passport at the Philippine Embassy. I must submit a thorough physical examination by a government-approved medical practitioner to secure a health clearance. Being a new graduate without professional work experience, getting a tax clearance from the Bureau of Internal Revenue (BIR) was smooth. Approval from the National Bureau of

Investigation (NBI) was also required, as was a police clearance. The need-to-do list seemed very daunting, and there were many forms to fill in. However, all those documents have to be obtained by me to be allowed to leave my country of origin and be admitted to my country of destination. My father gave me just enough money to defray all the expenses needed for transportation, food, and board and the processing of my travel documents. By my reckoning, I had just enough fees and no room for extras. I had spent five years commuting to and from school in Manila and nearby suburbs, so I was confident around Manila and its near vicinities. I patiently visited the relevant offices as I began at the top of my checklist.

I waited in line at the Philippine Embassy to apply for my passport. Mine was special since I was going abroad as a student and not as a tourist. The waiting was tedious; I had to be in line at the crack of dawn, even before the embassy opened, so I wouldn't have to stand way back in line. In more modern times, the process was made easy with the invention of the internet. An interested person could just go to the website, fill up the application online, send copies of documents online, and be given a date to personally appear at the designated time and place. But in my time, I had to get up very early, beat the traffic, and stand in line. It may be tedious and exhausting, but that was how things were done; all the requirements had to be accomplished within a specific time frame, or all efforts would be for naught. I could not leave the country, and my dreams would be gone like a puff of smoke.

As always, I stretched my patience while, with a bit of money in my pocket and a heart full of prayers, Manila remained my second home. I had to be able to cross out all the items in my need-to-do checklist one by one. With the grapevine alive with horror stories and rumors about having to grease palms (in the native tongue, "padulas" or to make slippery, or "lagay" or to put something) in every office so that papers would get processed, I was doubtful that I would be able to get all my papers processed on time. I needed more money for palm greasing, the rumored standard practice during that time if anyone wanted documents to be processed. It was a way of life that had come to be accepted, to give grease money to make the wheels of bureaucracy turn, to pass the red tape and get on the other side. Congress would later try to cut out a red tape by enacting a law, but that was still way in the future. With a prayer in my heart that I would not encounter this evil in the system, I set out to have my documents processed.

So, it was a massive surprise for me to find out that in every office I went to, there was somebody who was willing to help me who did not accept grease money. This was due to my being respectful, self-confident, and shy at the same time, which shone through and made people I met to respond to me positively. A person's innate good nature shines through, and people who discern it cannot turn away. People were impressed to know that I was going abroad on a scholarship grant from a top university and that I was offered work there at the same time. They were eager to assist this poor scholar who had studied hard for five years, graduated with honors, and was now given a huge break in his education and career. In every office I went to, word got around that I needed to get all my papers ready so I could go on with my journey to the University of California,

Davis. I was given a free ride, so to speak; no money to grease palms was demanded. I was not given the runaround and was entertained without delay. In a week, more or less, of my stay in Manila to get my papers ready, I got all the documents I needed duly processed, and I was relieved to be at last ready to go. I thanked my new acquaintances and my helpful "kababayans" (countrymen) at their respective offices for assisting me with enthusiasm and also thanked God for smoothing the way again for me. I was happy, it was 1963, and I was going to my destiny, the University of California, Davis, in the United States of America.

CHAPTER V

· · · · ·

Life in the Golden State of California

After my studies at the University of California, Davis, and the Heald Institute of Technology, also in California, I was on a hiatus for the purpose of applying for my green card. A green card is necessary to certify that I am indeed a permanent resident of the United States of America. If a person does not have a green card, he won't be able to work in America or do any business. So while waiting for my green card, I had to perform various odd jobs. I worked as a janitor and became a waiter in restaurants. I also worked seasonal jobs on farms, harvesting fruits and vegetables. Although harvesting fruits by hand was challenging work under the sun, I liked it for the bonus of being given a load of fresh fruits to take home. I learned to look for work like these that did not require a green card, but I had to be alert about it as the demand for workers was quickly filled. The pay was measly, but I needed it so I could sustain myself during this period of being unemployed in my professional capacity.

In 1965 the New U.S. Reform Immigration Laws opened for all the professional people of the world. After the announcement of these new laws, the Immigration Office was flooded with applications submitted by people owning diplomas in different fields. Day by day, the influx of professional people from all over the world arriving in the United States grew by leaps and bounds. They all hoped to find and partake of a slice of the American Dream. Many applicants needed a place to stay or had job offers lined up. There were some who were lucky to be able to find places to visit and jobs to work at. But many were not so fortunate. For them, the American Dream remained an unfulfilled dream, as elusive as wisps of smoke or always just beyond their grasp. Because of the difficulties they experienced in their new country, some gave up their applications and returned to their countries. If many went back home, many applicants decided to stay for better or worse. They endured hardship. They worked at odd jobs wherever and whenever they found them. Being aliens, they could not pick and choose jobs and were not paid much, but they hung on and never gave up on the better opportunities they hoped were waiting for them just around the corner. In a matter of five to ten years' time, more or less, these hard-working people were able to rise up from the ashes of poverty and achieve a measure of success in their newfound life. At last, the American Dream was theirs to live and revel in. Once again, industry and determination were their rewards.

• • • • •

CHAPTER VI

Getting a New Job in The United States of America

After an applicant for residency in the United States gets a Green Card, he can now reside permanently in the USA. And most of all, he can now apply for a job in his chosen profession if there be vacancies. If not, he can apply for a job he can or is willing to do. America is like Aladdin's cave of opportunities. Golden opportunities await those who are open and ready to reach them. Only your timidity and lack of confidence in yourself will limit your options, potential, and capabilities.

In contrast, in the Philippines, it is whom you know that will open doors for you. The "Padrino" (godfather or political/social sponsor or backer) system has become deeply rooted and has become the standard. An applicant can only get far if he has a political or social connection or backer, which is shameful. These "padrinos" or godfathers seek positions for people they wish to be employed from those they know are hiring in return for past favors or for the promise of future favors that may be asked of them. Those more deserving of the job are shunted aside in favor of those with connections or backers. But in America, what you know gets you in and puts your feet on the rung of the ladder of success. They do not suffer those whose qualifications are not suited to the job.

·····

CHAPTER VII

Finding my First Lady Love on the East Coast

After a few years of work in California, a good friend of mine who was living in Queens, New York, told me about a lady friend of his, who, to preserve her anonymity, I will name as Ms. Daisy, and for the same sense I am also giving my friend the fictitious name of Ted. My friend Ted, an engineer by profession, said she was a registered nurse, single, available, and very pretty. Would I get to know her or befriend her? He said she was working as a nurse in an exchange program. I had never entered the arena of courtship in my life. My life thus far has been spent studying hard to earn a degree during school semesters and working as a gardener during summers to make money to augment my school expenses and allowance. And then, I was offered an opportunity to further my studies and work in the United States. Being a serious and dedicated fellow, I focused keenly on the matters at hand, namely, my studies and work; these were separate from my attention. I did not have time to court a girl or even consider or look at a girl with a romantic view in mind.

For the first time in my life, I told myself why not? It was time I paid attention to other aspects of life, not merely studies and work. After all these years, I had become a highly educated scientist in agriculture, a much sought-after agricultural engineer who was an expert in my profession but needed much catching up in life as a young man. In the movie Camelot, King Arthur asks himself, "How to handle a woman? Do I flatter her? Do I threaten or cajole or plead? Do I brood or play the great romancer?" He was a great warrior king, but he was at a loss for handling a woman, his future wife—the same with me. I needed to be more knowledgeable about the courtship or dating process. The only women I encountered daily were my schoolmates, teachers, female relatives, and people around our neighborhood at home. I figured that at my age. It was time for me to take a dip in the dating pool. I was ready to meet women and participate in the dating scene. But first, I had to meet them and make myself available.

When I told my friend Ted I was interested, he gave me her telephone number. As always, when I decided on something, I quickly focused on it. I called her up and introduced myself as a friend of our mutual friend, Ted, who had given me her number. She said Ted had mentioned me to her several times, and he warned her that he had given me her number and that she should expect me to call any day. She was gracious and friendly when I rang and introduced myself. I asked if it would be alright for me to call her sometimes. I confided that even if I had lived for some time in the States, I would still get lonely and homesick, and talking to "kababayans" (countrymen) helps to cheer me up and chase away my longing to be in my own country and be with my family and friends. She agreed and said I could call her whenever she was not at work. So we began getting to know each other; I started by telling her that I was offered a scholarship and a job at the University of California, Davis. She said she earned her nursing degree from the University of Santo Tomas and came to the United States as an exchange nurse. She was working at the Columbia Hospital in New York City at the time of our acquaintance.

Daisy and I quickly became phone pals. We talked on the phone almost daily and called each other whenever we were off duty. Pretty soon, we were doing telebabad" every day. "Telebabad," a coined Filipino expression, is a combination of two words, "tele" for telephone and "babad," a Tagalog word which means to immerse. So "telebabad" means to be immersed in conversation with someone on the phone for a lengthy period. This went on for more than a year, and I slowly felt that our friendship was entering another level. My feelings for my phone pal had blossomed into more than mere friendship, and I suspected she might feel the same. The fact that we had never met was not a serious impediment to our friendship thus far. Our long hours of talking on the phone have made us feel that we already knew each other intimately. We opened up by telling each other details about our lives and ourselves, our likes and dislikes, our favorite things, and what we hope, dream, and aspire for. I felt my day was incomplete until I heard her voice on the phone. She could cheer me up and make my days turn out right. There was an inexplicable bubble of excitement within me that nothing could deflate like I was floating above the ground or walking on air because of this sheer feeling of lightness and joy. She always welcomed my calls, and I eagerly awaited hers. She said that she had told her family about me, and I replied that I had already told my family about her, and that was when I knew that this phone pal relationship was really becoming something serious. This is it: I was in love for the first time in my life, I had been hit by Cupid's arrow big time, and I didn't mind! I was delighted that she shared my feelings and didn't mind being my girlfriend!

CHAPTER VIII

• • • • •

When Two Hearts Decide they are Meant For Each Other

We agreed to meet at last in person. My first impression of her physical beauty, through the words of Ted describing her appearance to me and by hearing her on the phone, was spot on. She was a very pretty "morena" (brown complexioned) lady, although petit, only five feet tall, with dark brown eyes and long wavy hair. I also met her family, who were friendly and welcoming. Knowing that she and my family approved of our relationship, we realized that we were serious about our feelings and intentions for each other. It didn't take long for us to decide to take the leap and declare that we would like to commit ourselves to each other permanently, for the rest of our lives, as man and wife.

We began planning for the wedding. Earlier, I had already asked Daisy to marry me. I went down on one knee while I asked the fateful question, and she said yes enthusiastically without hesitation. I had no family then, so I was alone in the meeting with her family to ask for her hand in marriage. In the Philippines, this would be the

28

Filipino custom known as "pamamanhikan" (from the Tagalog word "panhik," which means to climb the stairs, the prospective groom climbs the stairs into his sweetheart's house to formally ask for her hand in marriage). Traditionally during the "pamamanhikan," the groom-to-be and his family meet with the bride-to-be and her family, usually in the bride's family abode, to formally ask for the bride's hand in marriage. This is also a way of showing that the prospective bride and groom respect and honor their parents by asking them to consent to their marriage and to bless their union even if both the bride and the groom are already of age and independent of their parent's financial support. On this occasion, the groom's family usually brings gifts and food to the bride's house to be partaken of after the rituals of the "pamamanhikan" have been observed, consisting simply of informing the bride's parents and those then present of the engaged couple's intention to marry and asking for their blessing and the giving of the same. It is an event eagerly anticipated by the engaged couples' families as it would allow them to meet and get to know each other before the wedding and plan the wedding details. These details would include, to name a few, the date of the wedding, the church where they would be wed, where the reception will be held, the theme and decorations, the couple's wedding attire, the honeymoon destination, whether there would be a "despedida de soltera" (literally translated from Spanish means goodbye to singlehood) for the bride and a stag or bachelor party for the groom, whether there would be a "sayawan" and "sabitan." "Sayawan" is the first dance of the bride and groom as a married couple, usually to their favorite love song. While they were dancing, their guests would pin money bills on their clothes. Sometimes tabs would be pinned on bills previously pinned by other guests, forming a long trail of money fluttering around the couple as they danced.

Depending on the financial resources of the groom's family, pigs, cows, goats, fish, and fowl would be slaughtered, butchered, gutted, and feathered for the "pamanhikan" feast. Every cook in the family would be busy chopping, stewing, marinating, roasting, frying, and baking to prepare their unique dishes. As I was alone, I bravely faced them all at Daisy's residence in Astoria, New York, and declared my honorable intentions.

We decided to tie the knot at Our Lady of Mount Carmel Catholic Church on June 25, 1969, a few days after Miss Gloria Diaz, the Philippines' bet to the Miss Universe contest, won the title. The Philippines won the Miss Universe crown for the first time, and I won the love of my bride I had hoped for forever. She looked charming, as a bride should in her gown and veil, as she walked down the aisle toward me. I was nervous and ecstatic at the same time, and I managed to utter my vows clearly and fervently. In no time, we were declared man and wife by the officiating priest. I proudly faced the assembled congregation and walked down the aisle together with my newly wedded wife on my arm. I felt like Prince Charming in a fairy tale I never wanted to end. Our reception was held at the Idyllic Room of the Rockefeller Center in New York City. Although none of the traditional Filipino engagement and wedding customs I mentioned were performed, we danced at our reception to our favorite song, "Unforgettable" by Nat King Cole. I was no longer alone in this vast country that has given me golden opportunities concerning my studies, career, and profession. Now I had a wife and an extended family, for I profoundly thanked God.

Before our marriage, we discussed practical matters such as where we would establish our residence, among other things. At that time, I worked in California while she worked in Astoria. We agreed that she would move to California, and we would live in my apartment there. Not long after the wedding, I noticed little changes in her. She was quiet and seemed to be sad. At first, I thought she was just a bit homesick, and, in time, she would get over it. We were yet in the first week of our married life, just at the beginning of the honeymoon stage of our marriage. I was looking at life with rose-colored shades and anticipating all the blissful things a newly wedded couple expects to share. But I observed that she had a gloomy air around her, and she was more downcast as the days passed. She was often in tears and on the phone talking to her family in New York almost daily. Her glum and despondent manner made me feel miserable and downhearted in the middle of our honeymoon, and I felt threads of tension form between us. I tried talking to her, asking her why she was melancholy and in tears, whether I did anything to offend her, and asked her forgiveness if I had. I tried to persuade her out of her dismal mood by offering things that might please her, like her favorite food and desserts, suggesting eating in restaurants or seeing sights like parks and beaches. I was very patient, loving, and sensitive to her moods, but soon, I had to admit that she did not seem happy living with me in California. Her melancholy mood continued, and this made me feel wretched and confused. I asked myself if I should leave my job and move to New York to please her. But I loved my job, and the weather where we lived in California suited me very well. New York was very cold in winter and stiflingly hot during the summer. We began to have arguments, mostly about her unhappiness living in California and wanting to be in New York instead. I felt that the woman that was my sweetheart was not the same woman who became my wife. Where did that charming lady go? I felt like I was trapped in a marriage to a stranger. After we were married, Daisy was able to get her green card. Due to the tension between us, I could not help but be resentful and think that maybe that is why she married me, to get a green card that would enable her to work as a nurse in the United States.

Despite her unhappiness and our arguments, we managed to start a family. Our first child, a girl, was born on December 14, 1971, our second child, a boy, was born on July 16, 1972 (and our third child, another girl, was born on January 18, 1977). I was so proud of being a father for the first and second time! It was like being entrusted with a sacred responsibility to care for these three souls who were my reasons for living, the font of my happiness, a commitment I joyously undertake. I did not mind the sleepless nights or the days when it was all I could do to stay on my feet in wakefulness. I learned what I could about formulas and feeding schedules, immunizations and vaccinations that are due, what to do in cases of colds, cough, or colic, the medicines and home remedies for bringing down a fever, shuffling with the babies around the house when they were learning their first steps. Pretty soon, they were learning their first words. The words "dada" and "mama" seemed to have been spoken by angels, my very own angels. In no time, they were singing the alphabet song, counting from one to ten, identifying shapes and colors, pointing to various objects around the house, and asking what that is, what it does, and why, lots of questions demanding answers. I loved all of it!

In seven years of marriage and despite having children in different stages of growth and development, my wife continued to pine for New York City. She never let go of her plans of going back to live and work there. I believed that with our brood, we would both be busy attending to their individual needs, and she would finally permanently forget about her desire to be back in New York. But that city seems to her to be like a magnet constantly exerting its pull on her. No amount of sleepless nights with kids crying because of wet or soiled diapers, of their being restless because of teething issues, or simply wanting to be fed or cuddled could make her ignore the allure or the siren call of New York City from her mind. After all these years, I felt desperate and helpless about how I could convince her to give up New York City. I started thinking about what to do and how to handle this ongoing problem that eight years of love, patience, and understanding could not resolve. The bitter rift between us was growing more comprehensive, but still, my wife would not budge because her family and friends kept encouraging her to move back to New York. She did not defend me when they would point out that I was still not financially well-off as they were, saying that I was only a poor farmer's son and not expected to attain high social status like their family. I was hurt to find out that they did not think of me as a worthy husband for Daisy and did not hold in esteem people like me who came from humble beginnings. I remember we had a very heated argument about this, and she was so incensed that she drew her wedding ring from her finger and threw it on the grass! That act rendered me speechless at that moment. I wondered if what she did was symbolic of her desire to get rid of me or that our marriage was something that had become oppressively burdensome that she would like to be rid of, too. How could she have forgotten our vows that we spoke before a representative of God who blessed and joined us in the sacrament of marriage? Did she even consider that her behavior and hard-headedness could have a detrimental effect on the lives of our children? I began thinking about the possibility of a divorce. But I did not want my children to experience the train-wreck impact of a divorce. They were more precious to me than all the wealth in the world, and their well-being will always be my priority. I will gladly deny myself the chance to achieve fame and fortune if that would have an unfortunate effect on their lives.

As the problem between us remained unresolved and because Daisy continued to be deaf to all my pleading and begging that we could be happy and enjoy a good life in California, I began to feel as if I was a nobody to her, someone she could ignore. I became silent and uncommunicative, especially when she was on one of her New York "telebabad" episodes. She was increasingly on the phone with her friends in New York, but, a woman named Nonette, who usually came to visit her in California. They would spend hours conversing, not minding the passing of time, not minding me either, as if I was not the man of the house, Daisy's husband. It was as if I was a ghost they could not see. I had no idea what they could talk about for hours on end. Being excluded made me feel like a dummy. I had no one to turn to for advice or company. I longed for someone to whom I could unburden myself, but I did not have friends close enough to trust and be my confidants. Some acquaintances may notice my misery and be careful to stay far in the background. I longed for my family to be there for me, but they were all in the Philippines then, and it would be some years before they could join me in the United States. All I could do was pray to God for wisdom and guidance to get me through the issues I faced.

Daisy began to go on short trips to New York. She traveled to New York when it pleased her to do so without even the courtesy of informing me of her plans. She often stayed there for extended periods. Then came when she decided to live there with her wealthy sister in New York and would visit me and the children in California only once a month. It made me a lonely and forsaken man to be deserted by my wife. The happiest place on earth for a wife should be beside her husband and her children, but I and our children were overpowered by the irresistible lure of New York City on my wife. I felt very sorry for myself and how things turned out to be between me and my wife. I wanted a family like the one I have in our small village in the Philippines, where my parents and siblings, and I happily lived despite being poor. Still, I resisted the idea of a divorce, thinking only of the ill effects that it would engender on our children. I did not lose hope that, somehow, our family would live together again in one place. I prayed to God that time would be sooner than expected and entrusted our fate to Him.

No matter what curveballs life throws at us, the wheel of life inexorably turns. I continued working in California while Daisy found a new nest with her wealthy, single sister in New York City. Maybe that was the life she craved, a life where she did not have to stick to a budget, like the life she had with me. I awaited her monthly visits hoping she would stay and forget about New York. But as the months passed, she said no such thing. For now, I told myself to accept the way things are and ditch the arguments against New York when she was around to make her visits worthwhile. I cannot save my marriage by nagging her to come back to us every time she visits. I was thankful that she came to visit at all. I allowed my tears to fall when I was alone to relieve the ache in my heart. I was as human as the next guy, and it was better to let the tears flow than drown my sorrows in alcohol. In life, one must pay his dues in the form of sacrifices; if that is what it would take to save my marriage, then I will gladly take up the yoke. My marriage is too precious not to fight for it. And after all the golden opportunities handed to me, despite being a poor farmer's kid living in a small village, I am prepared to fight for and protect all that is mine.

My destiny led me here in California to be a husband, among other things, to have a wife and children. I want my future to reflect in real life my desire to have a happy home life like the one I enjoyed in the bosom of my family in Cubao, where we loved and cared for one another and were all happy in each other's company. My achievements and successes in my education and life count as God's gifts, and I was just his vessel to manifest the wonder of his ways. He has blessed me abundantly by leading me along paths I never knew I could tread on and by bringing people into my life, my wife and children, to enhance it and fill me with joy. I am just a simple human with the same feelings and goals to survive in this beautiful world as everyone else. I have to go on with life; so precious and so beautiful! Nothing can stop me from doing so because I was destined to live that way. I came from a low-income family in my country, the Philippines, with my father, a farmer, my mother, housekeeper, and seven siblings.

We are a big family full of joy, happiness, and camaraderie. My coming to America was a miracle. They said God works in mysterious ways, as God did for me. (My story appeared in my other books: A TOUCH OF LIFE; and BEYOND FORGETTING (second edition), written ahead of this. Please keep track of them.) If you have a dream, never let it go. Embrace it with your heart. Nobody can grab that dream from you. It's yours. That's precisely what I did. And my God was by my side, working with me all along.

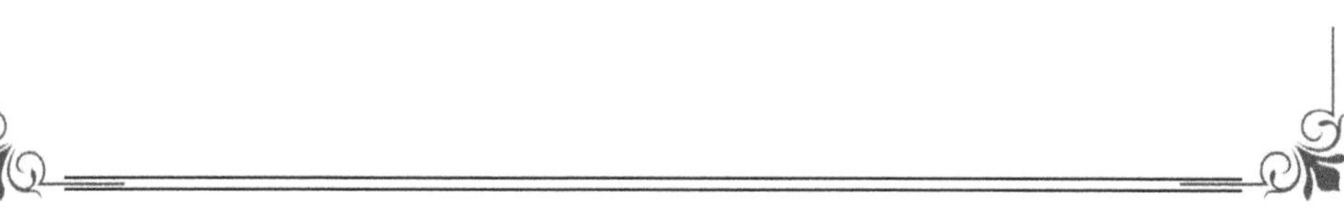

·····

CHAPTER IX

Daisy

Before the end of summer in 1977, my wife astounded me with news, one very good, one very bad. First, she told me that she was pregnant with our third child, a baby girl; I was going to be a father for the third time; what a blessing! I could not believe it at first. I thought it was just her ruse to convince me to come and live with her in New York. Before leaving for New York to live there, she told me there was no chance of her becoming pregnant again. Although pregnant, she did not want to see a doctor in California; she only wanted the OB/GYN in New York that her sister recommended. I was very excited that we were going to have another baby. Now to the terrible news. Now she was crying on the phone, and it alarmed me greatly that I was almost shouting at her, asking her what was wrong. She told me between sobs that she had undergone a test that confirmed that she had breast cancer. At that point, we were both crying while on the phone. I was shocked and grief-stricken to learn of her predicament. My first thought was, are we being punished by God for not giving in to each other's wishes which resulted in our estrangement as husband and wife? I was immediately sorry for where my thoughts led. I prayed to God that he might give us strength and courage to carry on amid this critical time. My mind could hardly deal with being pregnant and having breast cancer at the same time; the complications involved were beyond my reckoning. I felt my body numb, and the trauma the news brought was beyond description.

My wife's pregnancy and breast cancer simultaneously made my life more complicated and tiresome. I had to travel often to New York, on the East Coast, to attend to my wife's needs during her pregnancy and treatment and fly back to California, on the West Coast, where I had my job. I prayed to God to give me strength and good health to endure my current trials and carry out my responsibilities toward my family. My faith in Him helped me to keep up a brave front.

My wife and I were given choices by her doctors, whether to abort the baby and have a radical mastectomy to arrest the growth and spread of the cancer cells. She could only undergo one procedure at a time. If we choose to abort the baby, she would be able to undergo radical mastectomy at an earlier date. We decided to have the baby and have her experience the other procedure after she had given birth. We prayed for our baby girl's safe delivery and the operation's success on her breasts. The doctors explained that the radical mastectomy procedure required removing not only her breast but also the lymph nodes located at her underarm and the muscles on her chest wall.

Commuting from coast to coast was difficult, even at the best of times, but at that time, I was groaning under the burden of stress and anxiety over my wife's condition and having to take care of my children and work at my job. I had to go to my wife during her delivery of our youngest daughter and her radical mastectomy surgery after delivering the baby. It was time to talk to my boss about my situation and ask him for suggestions that might be of help. I believe that God worked another miracle in my favor when my boss found a position for me at a branch of our company located in New Jersey. I was overjoyed. Now I did not have to fly from coast to coast. The distance from New Jersey to New York was only about 71 miles and was accessible by plane, train, subway, ferry, bus, and car. The trip that would have taken hours was reduced to maybe 30 minutes to an hour, depending on where you're coming from and where you're going, and the travel cost was much cheaper. It eased my mind a lot to be a mere hour or so away at the most and then be on the other side of the continent. I'd have felt much better, though, if we lived in the same place under the same roof. So I gave up my apartment in California, packed up our belongings, said my goodbyes to my boss and co-workers, and moved to our new abode in New Jersey. However, my wife still preferred to live with her single sister, a doctor, in Astoria, New York City. I believe she chose to live with her sister because of her apprehension that I might be unable to support her medical needs financially. I admit that I did not earn that much then compared to her sister, a doctor, but we were not impoverished. I could support her and the kids, though maybe not in the style she wanted. To her and her side of the family, perhaps I was still a poor guy from the boondocks in the Philippines, and I doubt if that impression would ever be shaken off. My excellent educational record, which enabled me to earn a scholarship to one of the best schools in the United States, did not impress them. To them, the smell of the farm where I came was an aura that would always cling to me, which they would always find distasteful that even stateside air cannot dispel. Their attitude toward me was slowly poisoning our marriage because my wife was under their influence. She did not protest if they said those derogatory words against me; she allowed them to have their say anytime. Their words hurt me more than physical blows to my body, but I chose not to let that be known for the sake of keeping the peace. There was my wife with a critical and life-threatening condition and pregnant at the same time; I did not want to add to her emotional burdens. I wanted my presence to be a source of strength to her, a calming and peaceful influence, even if my heart was severely battered by how they disrespected me and took me for granted. I wanted her to understand that I would do everything for her and our coming child.

Ultimately, my wife succumbed to the onslaught of cancer at the end of summer in 1979. She was given all the treatments available, but the disease defeated all efforts. Maybe the fact that she deferred therapy during her pregnancy took its toll. We did all we could but could not keep her from being summoned to her heavenly home. When it was known that her end was near, she was taken by her family back to the Philippines, where she lived for a couple more weeks before she died. I knew that I would lose my wife, but still, I was not prepared for the devastation that I felt upon her passing.]

When Daisy died, so did my identity as her husband and father of her children end. My being ostracized by her family was complete and merciless. They did not consult me about her funeral, wake, or burial arrangements. They took everything out of my hands, including caring for my children. When my wife was still alive, my role as a husband and father of my children was preempted by her family. I could not do anything for my children without comments from them. I could not have time alone or indulge in bonding activities with them. I could not take them for an outing to the park or a meal at McDonald's; her sister would be vehemently against it. They would scream at my children if they expressed their desire to be with me or go anywhere. I wanted to vent my anger and resentment, but I could not for my wife's sake; I was afraid she might suffer a heart attack when she heard our voices raised in anger. They took my children into custody, never telling me about any of their plans or intentions for them. They completely ignored me if I asked or said anything, as if I had no right to speak or decide anything for my family. They talked amongst themselves, never including me in their circle. They made arrangements and decisions according to what they favored, totally excluding whatever preferences I may have.

I later learned of one of the reasons for their attitude toward me. It was the fact that I let them have their way when we were still in the States, the point that I would not say anything that might lead to arguments or fights. No matter what hurtful and insulting things they said about or against me, I just let those pass without a word of protest. I kept silent for the sake of my wife, who was lying on her sickbed. As I mentioned, I did not want to add to her worries and burdens. I wanted her to have calm and peaceful surroundings as possible. They must have believed I was a wimp of a man, insensitive to their verbal darts and jabs, and that they could run roughshod over me, especially since my wife did not say a word to defend me against them. They took advantage of my fear that my wife might take a turn for the worse if she heard us arguing or fighting, and they exploited that. I did not want to be blamed for my wife's worsening condition if I ever lost control of my temper. Now that my wife has passed away, they continued with that kind of attitude toward me. They did not allow me the last service I could do for my wife, which is to see to it that she be laid to rest according to our customs and traditions in her final resting place.

After my wife was buried, we continued with the "padasal," or nine days of prayer or novena for the deceased's soul. For nine days before the burial, the bereaved family and their relatives, friends, neighbors, and co-workers come together at the dead's house to participate in the novena offered for the eternal repose of the deceased's soul. The "padasal" is a solemn occasion and is not considered a social event, even if food or "merienda" (snacks) is offered. However, on the ninth and final day of prayer, a more varied menu is prepared depending on the financial resources of the bereaved family. For nine days, it would seem that our family was united, but only in prayer for my wife's soul, I was still treated as a pariah. Another gathering and memorial service occurred forty days after my wife's death. This tradition is based on the forty days it took for Jesus Christ to be resurrected from the dead. Of course, my wife was never coming back to us, much as I wanted to. Still, in our culture, it is believed that the deceased's soul remains on earth during this period of forty days to wander around their home and other places that they lived in when they were still alive before finally leaving this world and passing on to the next. Following tradition, our family and close relatives observed a mourning period for one year. We dressed in black for the first six months and later on wore clothes of a less blue shade, but no bright colors, until the year of mourning was over; although this dress code, so to speak, is less observed nowadays, the wearing of the mourning pin is preferred. The end of the year of mourning is called the "babang luksa"; it marks the first death anniversary of the deceased and puts an end to the wearing of mourning clothes. As before, our family and relatives, friends, neighbors, and co-workers gathered in a symbolic gesture of the end of our mourning. At that time, I felt that there would never be an end to my mourning for the loss of my wife; I missed her even if she preferred to leave apart from me and our children, and I needed time to get used to her passing. My children did not understand the absence of their mother. I tried to explain to them that their mother was now released from the suffering and pain she had endured because of her illness and that God, in His mercy, chose to grant her relief and peace by summoning her to heaven.

After my wife died, it was as if I had lost her and my whole family. My children were now firmly ensconced in the clutches of my wife's family and were hidden from me, and I felt that I could drown in my tears and sorrow and lose myself as well. As if treating me as a pariah was not enough, I discovered they did not put my name on my wife's death certificate. The space which should bear my name as her husband was left blank. I had to have that corrected because I needed that document when I returned to the United States.

Furthermore, the spaces were filled with fake names. Her parents' names are not Andong and Patsi, nor does she have a sister named Evelyn, and my wife's name was also incorrectly spelled. The doctor who signed the death certificate is a relative of theirs. I was horrified. I could only wonder what their reasons were for doing such a thing. Perhaps so that I could not find the document which I need to go back to the United States? What I had suffered at their hands would have indeed broken a lesser man. They have managed to make me appear as if I am a person with no feelings or identity, they have managed to separate me and my wife, and now they have managed to deprive me of my children. But I kept faith in God that someday all this pain and heartache would pass, and since He is a just and merciful God, He will see to it that justice will prevail. In the meantime, to them, I am a foolish fool who was quickly set aside and had my children's most precious things in his life taken from him without a fight. I was horrified at what they did with my wife's death certificate. Still, it also scared me into thinking that maybe they were plotting something more sinister against me, so I changed the date and time of my departure from the Philippines to feel even a semblance of safety.

They knowingly and willfully committed the crime of kidnapping my children. I tried to file a criminal case against my wife's family in the Philippines, even if I didn't know where they hid my children. At that time, I needed to return to the United States to report to work. Time, distance, and lack of funds derailed my plans to prosecute my wife's family, especially those who had taken custody of my children against my will and without my permission. I had to go back to work to earn a living. I could not afford to stay away from work for long periods. I could not afford the expense of traveling back and forth to attend hearings, and I could not afford to hire lawyers to handle the case.

Being heartbroken at the loss of my wife and my children being taken away from me and being helpless due to the combination of reasons of being unable to seek, pursue and obtain justice at my loss of custody of my children, I wondered if I had not yet plumbed the bottom of my despair. With a heart dripping with sorrow, I realized that I had to give up my pursuit of justice. My second wife convinced me to give up the fight for now. She said they will always be your children no matter where they are, and God will lead you all to each other's arms someday. I clung to that hope every day. I prayed to keep them safe and well. I prayed that they would not forget me and think kindly of me no matter how long we spent apart. I prayed that they would not forget the love I had shown them no matter how brief the time we were together. I prayed that they would understand that our being parted from one another was not my doing or decision and that I could never bear to be apart from them. So, I listened to my wife's advice. I had to go on living if I wanted us all to be reunited someday. I knew, in God's time, we would all meet again.

CHAPTER X

• • • • •

Moving On

Returning to the United States did not free me from the agony and gut-wrenching heartbreak that I suffered in the aftermath of all the drama and trauma that happened in the previous months. Losing your whole family is not something a person can quickly recover from. Soldiers are not the only prey of post-traumatic stress disorder (PTSD). War is not the only arena where people could suffer from anxiety and depression. I missed my wife even if she chose to live away from me while she was alive. I forgot my children and craved having them with me; I missed hearing their voices and having my arms around them. I fell into a deep, encompassing depression that I could not shake off or ignore. It would overcome me every hour of the day, no matter where or what I was doing.

The emotional misery would cripple me and leave me gasping for breath. At times I would think that I have finally overcome it, but I again would suffer another bout at its clutches. The severe loss of my family would envelop my being, throbbing and lingering for a long time. Anxiety and depression swirled around me like a dense fog that the warmth of sunlight could not banish. Later on, I realized that I should have talked to people about my problems piled on top of one another in tangles that I could not unravel. But I wouldn't say I liked to burden other people with my problems, so I kept everything to myself until I felt like I was drowning or going to break and be undone at any time. I realized that I should have confided in someone I could trust, in a friend, for that's what friends are for. It is wrong to keep every hurt or every heartache inside. Sometimes we cannot resolve or reason away what has hurt us by merely thinking about it. We should not say to ourselves that in time this too shall pass. Sometimes time does not pass fast enough for us to get over the things that hurt us or pose huge barriers for us to overcome. Time does not pass fast enough to at least dull the paralyzing ache of loss. When things are too much for us to keep up with, we must allow friends and family to take care of us and make things easier to endure or put up with. At the time of our suffering, it seems that we could not go on or that we could not forget the reasons that brought about our distress or even think about forgiving those who have caused this anguish. We must learn to dig deep into ourselves for reasons to even try to forgive or forget. Ultimately, we understand that it is a matter of choosing to live, get on with our lives, find meaning in them, give ourselves a chance at happiness, success, and fulfillment, or be crippled by pain, heartbreak, and bitterness. Having faith in God not only means that we believe in a loving and caring God, but having faith also means accepting all the tribulations that come our way, which is God's way of making us grow strong and mature in spirit. I had faith in God that he would help me reunite with my children someday, so I decided to leave the unfolding of this event in His own time. Forgiving is not easy to give, but it sets us free from the depths of misery. Letting go of the darkness and despair in our inner being to enjoy the light, love, and life. Forgetting does not mean we should ignore the suffering we endured. We must remember and be sure mine the events that led to our suffering and gather from them lessons that would teach and guide us as we move on in life so that we learn how to fight and defend ourselves from those who oppress us. We must learn how and whom to trust so that we can never be duped or taken advantage of by the unscrupulous. Foremost, we must learn to stand and speak up, insist on being heard, and pursue avenues in which our rights would be upheld and not be trampled upon or taken for granted. We have the right to be peaceful, we have the right to be joyful, and we have the right to choose to live life to the fullest, which is a God-given gift. "Forgive others not because they deserve forgiveness but because you deserve peace." Only my faith in God and prayers for his mercy and comforting love helped me to overcome my suffering. I prayed that God lift me and help me endure any trials that may come my way. To God be the glory forever.

CHAPTER XI

· · · · ·

Reunited

Twenty years later, in 1999, my three older children and I would be reunited in the United States. Being born in the U.S. made them U.S. citizens, and it was easy for them to return to where they should have been all this time, which is with me, their father. I welcomed them all with open arms, and my joy at their homecoming knew no bounds. They had all finished their studies in their respective professions. My eldest son, from my first family, is now an accountant, my second son, from my current family, is a civil engineer, while my two daughters are communication arts specialist and a pediatrician respectively. While they lived in the Philippines, I faithfully supported them financially and communicated with them without fail. Those days were when there was no Facetime, no video chatting, but good old snail mail and expensive overseas calls. But, of course, being separated by a vast ocean and living on different continents greatly impacted our relationship. A lot was lacking in our parent-child relationship; our day-to-day presence in each other's lives was the biggest thing. There were twenty years of unshared experiences and memories between my children and me, a huge yawning gap in my life. I missed their childhood and adolescent years and their coming into adulthood years. The loss of those years when I was not part of their growing-up years saddens and hurts me most deeply. I argue that the most precious things in life are not material things. Material things are convenient to own and possess, making life easier for us and contributing much to our comfort and leisure. The bling and sparkle that wealth can acquire may show the world how high our station in life has risen. They are not permanent. They are subject to the ebb and flow of fate and misfortune; in just a snap of your fingers, they're gone. People talk about the good old days and love to go down memory lane and reminisce about their childhood, their school days in grade school and up to their college years, their stint in the army, the early days when they were building up their careers, the people they've met and spent time with, their love life, what was the rage then in sports, music, movies, the political and economic climates and so on. I can spend hours with friends, former classmates, and siblings talking about those things about the good old days. But sadly, I cannot say anything about shared memories like those with my three older children during those twenty years we spent apart. When my siblings and our parents get together, we have a lot to talk about our life spent in Cubao. With so many children and so little money, misunderstandings happen, and quarrels erupt due to some imagined slight or perceived unfairness. Sometimes we managed to resolve things among ourselves. More often than not, our parents had to step in to dispense justice and discipline. They managed to do so with us children accepting chastisement, knowing they love us and only want what is best for us. With that understanding, we formed firm bonds with each other that became

stronger as we matured.

There was no parent-and-child communication between me and my older children. Twenty years of separation between me and my children has made us strangers. Twenty years of Christmases and holidays on my own until I had started a new family, twenty years of our birthdays spent on different continents, twenty years of pictures recording milestones they have achieved without me in them smiling widely and proudly. What are their favorite things to eat and things to do? What sports do they engage in, what types of movies and music excite or move them, what books do they read, and what kind of artworks do they admire? Who are their idols and heroes in real life, in fiction? Do they believe in gender equality, the elimination and destruction of nuclear weapons, and happily ever after? Who among them loves dancing, poetry, nature, cooking and baking, and doing chores around the house? Who among them is Doc, Sleepy, Happy, Grumpy, or Bashful? The nitty gritty knowledge of a parent about their children, on how they think, react, or respond to things and situations, that is personally learned by living with them over the years; that is what the selfishness and arrogance of my wife's family have deprived me of. Of course, this goes both ways; I am their father, who is also a stranger to them. They share my flesh and blood, and they, as members of the next generation of the De La Rosa clan, are part of our lineage. Do they wonder about this person they call Papa, who supported them financially, wrote them letters, and spent a small fortune on expensive overseas calls to hear their voices? But who is he? What makes him tick? Is he gentle and kind-hearted, is he wise and respectable, is he loving and understanding, is he cheerful and fun-loving? Is he serious and God-fearing? Does he give a damn about the environment and saving planet Earth? If I told them how I ached for them to be with me all those twenty years, would they believe me? Would they believe me if I told them how desperately helpless I was when they were stolen from me? Did those who stole them from my custody tell them falsehoods about me or mislead them about the way they happened to live with my wife's family and not with me?

I was determined that they should know the truth about what happened between me and my wife's family before and after their mother died. I did not want them to think ill or less of me through no fault of mine. I wanted to address the matter immediately and set my mind to rest. My narration, though, was greeted with much less warmth than I anticipated. They listened to me respectfully but were unanimously silent. They did not seem to grasp the mental anguish that I suffered all those years when they were in the custody of their mother's family. I needed them to know the truth and believe in it. I understood then that although they would not refute my revelation, they were unwilling to take sides. They harbored loyalty toward those who raised them and cared for them for twenty years, which they considered their immediate family for so long. I hoped that they would mull over what I revealed and bother to take steps to check and verify my chronicle of that dark part of my life and soon recognize the truth of my words. There is no greater love than a parent's love for their children. Now that my older children were back with me, I rejoiced with all my heart, thanked God for this reunion, and prayed that we might never be parted again. Being reunited with my children made me resolve to leave the dark past behind and begin a new life with my complete family.

In a manner of speaking, I was determined to forget all the hurt that I suffered, my humiliation at the disrespect that my first wife's family had shown me. With all the academic honors bestowed on me and my achievements thus far, I never thought I would be a victim of such bias and prejudice. The family of my older children's mother looked down on me for being the son of a poor farmer. They forgot that He who redeemed us from sin was the son of a poor carpenter. As if we could bring our accumulated wealth, trophies, and bling with us when we die, our souls have to stand before God and await His judgment. "The first step towards heaven is to find the worth of your soul (Bishop Ryle)." We must know how to surrender our stony heart and have a heart that trusts and submits to God.

"For what has a man profited if he shall gain the whole world and lose his soul? (Matthew 16:26)". I have seen how domineering and high-handed they are that I should have realized how futile it is to expect them to change their ways. In their mind, their wealth and societal position have given them a license to be judgmental and condescending toward a person of humble roots like me. I cannot do anything about them and their attitude or change them. I can only change myself to better myself and not open myself to bad karma by emulating them. And I am sure that bad karma is the fate that will beset those who have acted against the teachings of God, who has urged us to do only what is good in order to save our souls from eternal damnation. For those who are willing to be loyal to the word of God and sacrifice to look for the gate and the narrow way which "leadeth unto life" and be among the "few there be that find it," the reward is the "vaulting ambition" prospering and coming to fruition. And could the result of their unsuccessful aspirations and goals be strife and the breakdown of harmony among them? I don't know since I am not part of their circle, but I cannot help but hear what little birdies chirp and Twitter about here and there. "For everything, there is a season and a time for every matter under heaven… (Ecclesiastes 3)." With my elder children's homecoming, my time to laugh and rejoice has come, and for others who have let themselves be the prey of bad karma, their time to lose and weep is now.

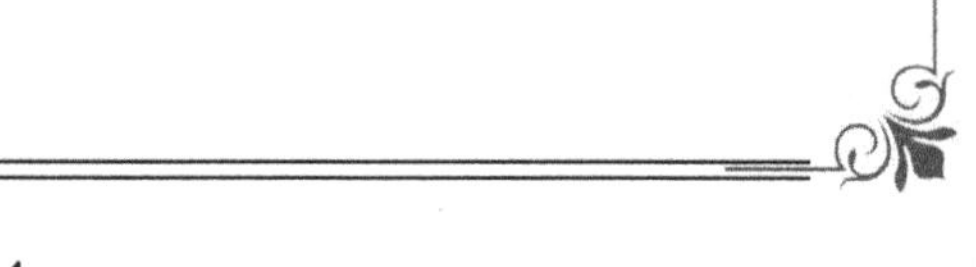

CHAPTER XII

· · · · ·

Some Unforgettable Memories of Life in The United States of America

More than a year had passed since my first wife had demised when I happened to be at my Aunt Genevieve's house in New Jersey to attend a party. I was living in New Jersey then, and my aunt, who would be starting her new job in a nearby city, was on vacation to visit friends and relatives. She introduced me to some friends of hers whom I had not yet met. One particular lady looked very special to me, and I kept thinking about her. Her name had a heavenly ring to it, Mary. My aunt rang me later that night after I went home. She said she had something to tell and was sure it was wonderful news for me. "Quicoy, she said, "I have a surprise for you today; I know you're going to like it, and you will love me forever for it." I replied, "What is it, Auntie Genevieve?" She said, " Remember that beautiful lady at the party tonight? She is the niece of your Tia Rose, the wife of Atty. John V." "Yes, Auntie, I remember her," I said, "I was just too shy to talk to her." "She is pretty, isn't she?" Yes, Auntie, she certainly is." Then

Auntie Genevieve said, "I want you to court her. When you do, I'm sure you will forget all your loneliness and all other troubles that you may have after the death of your wife, Daisy." Aunt Genevieve's concern touched me. She knew very well how much I grieved over the death of my wife and losing custody over my children due to my in-laws' underhanded shenanigans. Again, I felt that familiar pang washes over me as the memory of my trauma was again refreshed. It seemed then that I could never stop crying; the pool of grief I had fallen into seemed bottomless. I had nobody to lean on then except Auntie Genevieve because my parents and siblings still resided in the Philippines. She was my rock and tireless in supporting me to keep me going. She took on the role of our clan by always being there for me whenever I needed comfort and moral support. I also sought refuge in prayer and my faith in God, trusting him to give me strength and to guide me out of my misery. But Auntie Genevieve was a solid presence during those dark days when I lived at home in a foreign land. So now, my aunt believed that an attractive lady would distract me from my hopelessness and solitude. I believe that God, in His perfect timing, had used my aunt's party to introduce a person in my life who would attract me and bring me newfound happiness. I smiled to myself. Not a bad idea since she captured my attention as soon as I saw her at the party that evening. To me, she looked much like Michelangelo's famous painting of the Mona Lisa. Like the subject in the painting, Mary (what a holy name!) had straight, silky hair flowing freely down her shoulders. I was a budding photographer in those days. I would become a professional photographer for decades later, and I very much wished that an opportunity would present itself for me to be able to take a photograph of her. I gave it a few days of thought, and during a weekend, I gathered enough boldness to pick up the phone and dial the number given to me. My nervousness heightened; after all, it had been quite a few years since I had asked any woman for a date. The phone rang four or five times before it was picked up. I heard a sweet voice say hello. I said, "Hello, is this Miss Mary Grace?" The sweet voice replied, " Yes, this is she speaking." I introduced myself as Frank, the nephew of Aunt Genevieve. I asked how she was, and she answered she was doing fine. And then, I asked her if she had time to go for a stroll with me down at a nearby park and later have lunch together. She accepted my invitation and said it was her pleasure to walk on a beautiful autumn day. At the park, when I expressed my pleasure at her acceptance of my invitation, she told me that my Aunt Genevieve and her Aunt Rosing had told her many things about me. I told her I hoped they only had good things to say about me, and she said they did. I learned that she temporarily lived with her Aunt Rosing before she was given a Green Card and became a resident. Her Green Card meant she was granted authorization to live and work in the United States permanently. She revealed that she had passed the State Accounting Examinations and had been lucky to find a good job in New Jersey as an auditor. Back home in the Philippines, she worked as a Certified Public Accountant. She had already found herself an apartment in New Jersey. "I'm so happy for you, Miss Mary Grace," I said, my nervousness manifesting in my stiff formality. It must have made her uncomfortable because she said, "Just call me Mary Grace. By the way, I feel comfortable that way." So, I replied, "Just call me Frank or Paco." It was lunchtime by now, and I spotted a Roy Roger's Restaurant just nearby, and we headed toward it. I asked her if she liked fried chicken, and she said she loved it. We ordered a family box and everything to go with it and enjoyed eating our chicken. After lunch, we spent the afternoon taking pictures in the park with my camera and had a couple of shots of us together as souvenirs. (***do you still have those photos?) Autumn brings out various beautiful vivid colors of nature, with the leaves of trees turning from the verdant greens of summer into shades of yellow and gold, orange, and russet, red, purple, and brown. I suppose nature puts up this show of colors before the trees become "bare ruined choirs where late the sweet birds sang" and covers the land with the shimmering white of winter snow. We stayed at the park until late afternoon, talking, getting to know more about each other, and enjoying the autumn atmosphere. It was getting cold, leaves were falling from the trees, and there were a lot of dried leaves scattered beneath our feet; there might even be frost on the ground the next morning, but the aspect of the place did not seem to be dreary. The chill in the air was bracing, and the company was pretty and inspiring. Good things must end, so they say, and the time has come for us to part ways, just for the day. I thanked her for spending time with me and said I enjoyed her company immensely. She said that she enjoyed the day, too. I promised to call her again soon, and she said she hoped I would.

CHAPTER XIII

• • • • • •

My Family from My Country Arrived in New Jersey

After the death of my first lady love, I had to return to the United States on my own since my children were literally kidnapped by my wife's family and were kept away from me. I did not then have the financial capacity to file proceedings against them, and since I had to get back to work, I did not have time to file cases in the Philippines and attend to them myself. I also wanted to spare my children from the rigors and trauma of being the bone of contention, so to speak, between myself and their maternal relatives. I consoled myself with the knowledge that they would be in good hands; they would be well cared for and provided for by my first wife's family. With a heavy heart, I returned to the United States to resume my job obligations. I decided to permanently transfer my residence to New Jersey and not return to California. In 1979, the plans of my family to immigrate to the United States were hastily coming to pass, so I bought a new house to accommodate everyone. It was a seven-bedroom house situated on an oversized lot.

I intended to turn the spacious yard into a garden. I did gardening a lot when I was a boy in Cubao. One of my chores was to tend to my father's vegetable garden, and he taught me quite a lot about planting and growing plants. The house also had the advantage of being accessible to bus routes so that anyone who did not have a means of transportation could quickly get a ride by bus. My office was in Murray Hill, New Jersey, only fifteen miles (24 kilometers) from my Union County residence, about an easy thirty-minute drive even in winter. I was fortunate to keep the same job that I had in California; sometimes, relocating would force a person to accept a lower position and less compensation. My former boss was very understanding when I told him that I had to be near my sick wife, and he helped me look for a position at our offices nearest to New York, where my first wife was residing with her sister during her battle with cancer.

I barely had time to prepare the house for the arrival of my clan. They arrived one after another, twenty-four of them, i.e., mother, brothers and sisters, in-laws, and nephews & nieces.

Oh, my own big and lively family was included here! Wow, what beautiful chaos it was! With so many of us, we had to devise tight arrangements to fit into our cozy seven-bedroom house. But you know what? We made it work, and it became our very own bustling haven.

Every day was filled with joy and excitement as we embraced our new lives in a foreign country. It felt like a never-ending celebration, as if every day was a party waiting to happen! But as they say, good things don't always last forever. Our desires and preferences naturally started to clash with each of us being unique individuals. Suddenly, we found ourselves in a situation where we had to ask, "Who's in charge here?"

I can handle herding a thousand sheep, but trying to manage the needs and wants of twenty-four family members was a whole different challenge! Can you imagine the chaos? Everyone wanted a piece of the American dream, and who could blame them? Denying anyone that opportunity wasn't an option.

So we decided to buckle down, roll up our sleeves, and work together to make it happen. We knew that success would take a lot of work, but that didn't deter us. We were determined to carve out our slice of that delectable American pie.

And you know what? We did it. Through sheer perseverance and a shared commitment to our goals, we managed to overcome the hurdles. Our family became an embodiment of resilience, and we learned that when we stand together, there's no challenge we can't conquer.

So, here's to our incredible family and the memories we made together. We may have faced obstacles along the way, but those experiences shaped us into the strong, united force we are today. Cheers to our unwavering spirit and the belief that hard work pays off.

CHAPTER XIV

• • • • •

The Immigrants

"Work hard! Make it happen! For us to achieve our dreams and secure our piece of the American Pie, let's get the ball rolling. I need everyone's attention, please. For us to work together effectively, you must listen to me. For now, I'll be taking on the role of the boss within this household.

Those of you who are legally able to work, I want you to go out and find a job. As soon as you step outside the threshold of this house, start knocking on the doors of businesses in search of employment. Keep doing it persistently until you find one. And if you fail initially, don't lose hope. Take a trip to NYC, just half an hour away by bus. Remember, you all have Green Cards, so use them as your identification wherever you go. Bring along your address and telephone number as well. Apply the same strategy: knock on every door until you find a job. In no time, you will secure employment.

Once you have a job, give it your all and work hard. Save your money diligently. If you accumulate enough funds, start looking for an apartment or a temporary place while establishing yourself in this

new country. Don't be too selective or picky at this stage. You can have all the luxuries later when you're more stable. I've been through this process and eventually needed to remember how I started. Life is a cycle, and that's just the way it goes. Keep your faith strong and maintain a smile on your face. Every day is an adventure waiting to be enjoyed.

So let's embrace this journey together, face the challenges head-on, and make the most of every opportunity that comes our way. Remember, hard work, determination, and a positive attitude will pave the way to our American Dream. Let's go out there and seize it!"

Wow, after delivering that heartfelt lecture to your family, your house has become empty, leaving just you, your wife, and your son, Glen, in a once bustling seven-bedroom home. Life can take unexpected turns, can't it? But fear not, my dear readers, for the story is far from over. So please, bear with me as we continue this journey together.

Before moving to Florida, I extended a warm invitation to my newfound friend, Mary, to visit my new home in New Jersey and my entire family from the Philippines. It was a surprise for Mary, and we planned to make it a memorable weekend since we were all off from work.

We prepared an abundance of delicious Filipino food and drinks, including a whole pig skewered on a bamboo pole and roasted over burning charcoal for about six hours. The pig had been marinated overnight with a blend of traditional Philippine spices and local

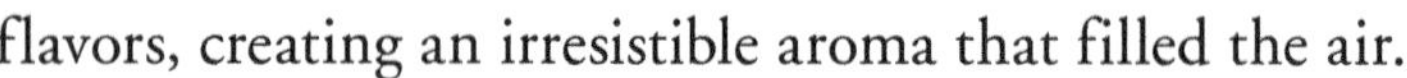

flavors, creating an irresistible aroma that filled the air.

On Saturday, everyone in my household worked diligently in the kitchen. The day was a whirlwind of activity, both inside the house and outside. It felt as if we were preparing for a grand wedding celebration. The atmosphere was bustling with excitement and anticipation.

Despite the approaching winter, the day was remarkably beautiful and breezy. Our whole neighborhood seemed to notice the buzz of activity emanating from our home. The enticing aroma of the roasting pig on the open fire traveled through the air, captivating the senses of those nearby. It was as if the scent alone could beckon you to come closer and join in the festivities.

The preparations continued throughout the day as laughter, conversations, and rattling pots and pans filled the space. The spirit of togetherness and camaraderie was evident, and the aroma of the delectable food created a sense of anticipation among us all.

Around noon, our awaited visitor arrived from Jersey City, and to her pleasant surprise, she wasn't taken aback by the bustling crowd. I had already informed her about the lively gathering that awaited her. As she approached the house, a colorful welcome sign greeted her, showcasing the warmth of our hospitality. Even the newly arrived immigrants joined in to make her feel at home.

We decided to set the dining table outdoors, right in the heart of our garden. The table was adorned with banana leaves sourced from Florida, creating an authentic and vibrant touch. Encircling

the table were ripe tomatoes, freshly picked from our garden in NJ. These tomatoes were known for their unrivaled sweetness and added flavor to the atmosphere.

At the center of the table stood the star of the feast, the whole roasted pig, skillfully pre-sliced and ready to be devoured. Sauces and condiments were thoughtfully placed around the table, ensuring everyone had easy access to enhance their culinary experience. Surrounding the succulent pig were a variety of Filipino dishes, such as grilled prawns, shrimp, bangus (milkfish), BBQ chicken, BBQ baby back ribs, grilled corn on the cob, spring egg rolls, and an assortment of vibrant salads. Steaming rice bowls, a Filipino cuisine staple, accompanied each dish.

In the background, melodic and enchanting music from the Philippines filled the air, creating a delightful ambiance. Those who felt the rhythm in their souls couldn't resist the urge to dance, swaying to the beats of their homeland. Despite the late autumn breeze, the atmosphere in my beloved garden remained cozy and welcoming, even with fallen rose petals scattered on the ground.

Everyone savored the delicious food, indulging in the flavors that reminded them of home. Laughter and lively conversations echoed around the table as bonds were formed, and memories were shared. The roasted pig vanished quickly, devoured by eager appetites before we even could slice the welcome cake!

CHAPTER XV

· · · · ·

Planning to Move to Sunny Florida

After a year of courtship, Mary Grace and I found our hearts intertwined, leading us to the sacred vows of marriage. On November 23, 1979, our souls became one as we exchanged vows at Saint Michael's Church in Cranford, NJ—the esteemed Msgr. Torrecampo officiated the ceremony, surrounded by our loved ones.

Dr. Alcantara stood by my side as my best man, while Ms. Celeste graced the occasion as the maid of honor. Mr. and Mrs. Vega, dear friends, and supporters, joyfully took on the roles of sponsors. After the ceremony, we celebrated with a reception at Le Affaire Restaurant in Springfield, NJ. It was a joyous affair, filled with laughter, music, and the company of cherished family and friends.

As we embarked on our journey as a married couple, my new wife and I decided to find a new home in our familiar neighborhood. We settled on a cozy two-bedroom house ideally suited for the three of us. Despite its modest size, the house offered ample space and was surrounded by the natural beauty of a giant cherry tree and a cluster of sugar maple trees in the backyard. Its proximity to NYC and convenient transportation options at every corner made it an ideal location. We fell in love with the house, appreciating all its amenities and the welcoming neighborhood that embraced us.

However, as life unfolded and time marched on, we began contemplating a change in our environment. The busy and congested city life, coupled with the harshness of winter and the inevitable effects of aging on our physical bodies, led us to consider a move to sunny Florida. Florida's milder climate enticed us, offering respite from the harsh winters we had grown accustomed to in NJ. We cherished the beauty of snow and the wonders of winter, but there came a point when we realized the need for a different environment and weather. We recognize that we can make such choices and adapt to new surroundings.

We had experienced numerous winters in NJ, some filled with enchanting beauty while others brought challenges. We understood that we have little control over the circumstances of the world. Instead, we chose to embrace the changes, adapt ourselves to new surroundings, and find joy in every season. Such is how God has created the Earth, with its ever-evolving nature and diverse experiences.

CHAPTER XVI

• • • • •

Another Big Move to The Sunshine State, The Vacation Capital of The World

As the decision to move to Florida excited my son, Glen, and my new wife, Mary, we took the necessary steps to facilitate the transition. We enlisted the services of a professional moving company to handle the packing and transportation of our household belongings. They meticulously labeled each box, ensuring a smooth and organized unpacking process upon our arrival in Florida. We aimed to keep things simple, avoiding confusion during the unpacking phase.

With everything in order, we prepared for the closing of our house in New Jersey. Tomorrow would mark the finalization of this chapter in our lives. Today, the movers would arrive to pick up all our belongings, readying them for their journey to our new home in Florida. To make the process more convenient, we made a reservation at a nearby hotel where we would spend the night. The following morning, we would drive to Florida, bidding farewell to New Jersey.

As we said our goodbyes to New Jersey, we expressed gratitude for everything it provided us. Our resources, opportunities, and the slice of the American Pie we had enjoyed all came from this place. It has played a significant role in shaping our lives and granting us the chance to pursue our dreams. We carried those experiences and memories with us as we set off on this new adventure.

CHAPTER XVII

• • • • •

Welcome to The Sunshine State of Florida! Here We Come!

The journey from New Jersey to Florida covered approximately 1,200 miles, taking us around eighteen hours of driving time. We stopped in South Carolina for a night's rest, breaking up the long drive. Despite the duration, the scenic views along the way kept us entertained, and the presence of our curious seven-year-old son added an extra layer of excitement. He marveled at everything he saw along the highways, his curiosity bringing a sense of wonder to the journey. My wife took care of him, ensuring he remained comfortable and engaged while keeping an eye on me to prevent drowsiness during the extended drive.

I sometimes felt my eyes grow heavy, but I resorted to various tactics to stay awake. Squeezing my ears and turning up the radio's volume helped combat the fatigue to some extent. As we continued our drive and passed through the state of Georgia, the realization that we were drawing closer to Florida filled me with anticipation. However, as my wife and son succumbed to sleep, I found myself alone on the highway, surrounded by the vastness of the road. The clear blue skies stretched endlessly, with vegetation adorning both sides of the road. At that moment, a sense of eternity washed over me, causing me to contemplate the vastness of the world and beyond.

Thoughts of heaven and the incomprehensibility of our perception of the world filled my mind. How can we truly grasp the mysteries around us and in the realms beyond? I pondered these questions, realizing that sometimes the best approach is to leave things as they are, embracing the wonder and accepting the limits of our understanding. Curiosity may drive us, but aspects of life and existence may remain beyond our comprehension.

......

CHAPTER XVIII

We've Arrived

With the excitement of settling into our new home in Florida, we embraced the milder winter climate and the lush green surroundings. Although the absence of bare trees and the flat terrain differed from our previous experiences, we found solace in the comfort and tranquility of our new residence. Our small but spacious four-bedroom house is nestled among the shade of tall trees, providing a serene atmosphere in a developing neighborhood.

February gradually transitioned into warmer yet cool Florida weather as we took our time organizing and arranging the furniture and interior decorations. The absence of snow and the perpetually green surroundings delighted us. With most household items in place, we decided it was time to celebrate our new beginning as a family of three. Our first dinner in the new house marked a significant milestone, and we savored the moment with gratitude.

After ensuring we were well-rested and settled, we treated our son to a memorable adventure at the Magic Kingdom in Walt Disney

World, a short drive away in Orlando. The joy and wonderment on our son's face reminded us that no matter our age, there will always be a child within us. As we embarked on thrilling roller coaster rides and faced our fears head-on, we realized that embracing life's excitement and unpredictability can bring profound joy. Even at eighty-five, I affirmed that experiencing such exhilaration is preferable to a mundane existence.

As spring approached, we observed the evergreen beauty of Florida's landscape, missing the vibrant blooms of our New Jersey garden. The early blooming crocuses, daffodils, and tulips held a special place in our hearts, and we fondly reminisced about the colorful display they once provided. However, we acknowledged that new opportunities awaited us in Florida, and we were far from retirement age.

With the realization that quitting our previous jobs made us ineligible for unemployment benefits, we faced the challenge of finding new employment opportunities. Due to our experience and age, the job prospects seemed bleak. This circumstance led us to consider starting our own family business. While uncertain of the outcome, we weighed the risks and deliberated on the possibilities. Despite lacking business experience in our new location, we believed that with determination, prayer, and my wife's expertise as a Certified Public Accountant, we could navigate the uncharted territory.

Encouraged by our faith and determination, we embarked on a new venture—a convenience store and fast food-to-go establishment. After securing a favorable location in a newly opened shopping area near our home, we swiftly made progress, signing a contract and arranging for the necessary permits, licenses, and equipment. As we called various suppliers and started procuring merchandise, we also began assembling a team consisting of a cook, a cashier, and a helper.

While the journey was demanding and required meticulous planning, we took solace in the knowledge that we were progressing toward our entrepreneurial dreams. The support from the people around us eased our concerns, and we remained hopeful as we prepared to open our doors for business. The road ahead was uncertain, but we were ready to face the challenges, armed with determination, faith, and the belief that taking a chance on our dreams was a gamble worth pursuing.

CHAPTER XIX

· · · · ·

Store Opening

Our Family Convenience Store Plus grand opening in March of '88 was met with excitement and anticipation. Our dedicated team arrived early to ensure everything was prepared for the influx of customers. To attract attention, we offered a promotional deal of one free Spring Egg Roll and a small drink to entice new patrons. The lively music played to create a vibrant atmosphere that would catch the attention of passersby.

However, we soon encountered unexpected challenges due to the store's location. Situated across from the local Elementary School and Southwest Junior High, the store became a hub of activity during school opening and closing times. The bustling corner was filled with eager children, posing a significant challenge in managing their influx during peak hours. Despite our best efforts to prevent children from taking items without paying proved nearly impossible, leading to financial strain and potential bankruptcy.

We recognized the importance of discipline starting at home and understood that children would be children. We sought solutions

to address this issue, seeking assistance from the police and school principals. Unfortunately, our efforts yielded limited results. The convenience store's location seemed ill-suited for our needs and being the first occupant in a new building in a developing area added to our predicament.

It became evident that the constant theft and loss of merchandise were untenable, and we faced the difficult decision to find a solution to this ongoing challenge. As we navigated this unexpected hurdle, we contemplated potential remedies and explored alternatives to enable us to continue our business without compromising our financial stability.

The situation underscored the importance of careful consideration when selecting a business location and assessing its suitability for the target market. While this endeavor had proven challenging, we remained determined to find a resolution and persevere in our entrepreneurial journey.

CHAPTER XX

· · · · ·

We Lost It

What happened next was even more terrible. After we closed the store in 1993, my wife fell seriously ill. It was a devastating blow for us. We were in a difficult situation with no insurance and very little money. Our 12-year-old son was attending school, and the vacant store needed to be cleaned before we could hand it back to the owner. We reached out to some relatives, hoping they would be able to lend a helping hand, but to our dismay, they turned their backs on us. It was a heart-wrenching realization of how cruel the world could be—a concept I struggled to comprehend.

The store was a substantial space, spanning 2500 sq. ft., and there was an immense amount of work to be done. Cleaning every nook and cranny and removing all the shelving and equipment seemed like an impossible task. However, with the kindness of some of our good neighbors, we managed to accomplish the daunting job. Together, we put in our best efforts and transformed the once cluttered and dusty store into a clean space.

To make matters worse, we had a surplus of groceries that needed to be taken care of. Determined not to let anything go to waste, we advertised the items and worked tirelessly to sell them all within a week. It was by the grace of God that our efforts paid off, and we could sell everything. His divine intervention was evident during that challenging time, reminding us that He always finds a way to help His creations in need.

During this trying period, I couldn't help but observe the inherent tendency of people to distance themselves when someone is in trouble. It was a bitter truth that resonated with me. However, despite the disappointment, I realized that we must always hold onto hope and have faith in a higher power. God's persistent presence and assistance showed me that even in the face of adversity, a greater plan is at play.

We picked ourselves up, grateful for the support of our neighbors and the blessings bestowed upon us. Although we couldn't rely on the assistance we expected from our relatives, we learned to trust in the kindness of others and the resilience within ourselves. The experience left an indelible mark on our lives, reminding us of the importance of empathy, compassion, and the unwavering faith that carries us through the darkest times.

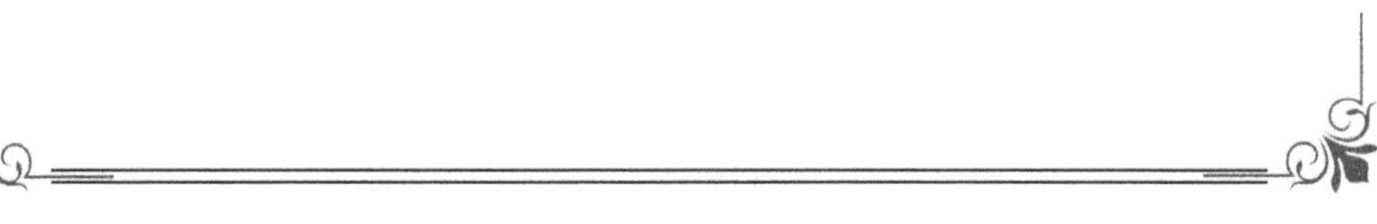

CHAPTER XXI

• • • • •

Somebody Call 911

We were left in the dark, unsure of what could be causing my wife's relentless vomiting. Determined to find answers, I rushed her to the emergency room, hoping the medical professionals could shed some light on her condition. The hospital was conveniently located close to our house, a prominent institution within the community.

The following morning, we received a visit from a neurosurgeon named Dr. John P. He exuded a sense of confidence and warmth, with an aura that reflected his experience and character. It felt as though he might be the answer to our prayers. Dr. John P. introduced himself to my wife and me, and we were instantly pleased to meet him.

Without wasting time, Dr. John P. gathered the medical reports and lab results, ready to unveil the findings. As he began to speak, he informed us that the MRI had revealed a sizable tumor atop the pituitary and hypothalamus glands in my wife's brain. It was the size of a golf ball, and surgery couldn't be delayed. We faced a critical decision, and there was no time to seek a second opinion.

Overwhelmed with fear and uncertainty, we turned to prayer, seeking guidance from the divine. We trusted that the doctors were mere instruments of God's will and that He would guide us through this ordeal.

My wife and I closed our eyes with heavy hearts, sending our prayers heavenward. We found solace in our faith and belief that God works through the hands of skilled physicians. Ultimately, we aligned ourselves with Dr. John P. and agreed that the surgery must be performed immediately. The procedure was invasive and incredibly delicate, with the looming risk of damaging the optic nerve. The tumor had grown so much that my wife's vision would likely be affected, rendering her legally blind. She could only perceive tunnel vision, making driving an impossibility.

The gravity of the situation weighed heavily upon us, but we remained steadfast in our faith, clinging to the hope that the surgery would bring about a positive outcome. Our trust in God's plan gave us the strength to face the uncertainty ahead. We entrusted my wife's life to the skilled hands of Dr. John P., acknowledging the risks involved and believing in the potential for healing and restoration.

As we braced ourselves for the challenges that awaited us, we knew that this journey would test our resilience individually and as a family. Little did we realize that this trial would also serve as a testament to the power of love, faith, and the unwavering determination to overcome any obstacles life throws our way.

CHAPTER XXII

· · · · ·

The Diagnosis

With the first surgery behind us, we felt relief and hope. However, our optimism was short-lived. My wife underwent several procedures the day after the surgery to assess her condition. To our dismay, the lab results revealed a blood clot in her brain. The doctors informed us that a second surgery was necessary to remove the clot. It was a devastating blow, another hurdle to overcome. There was no alternative but to proceed with the surgery. We were left grappling with feelings of fear and uncertainty once again.

The second surgery commenced, and my heart ached as I waited anxiously for news of its outcome. When my wife was finally brought back to her room, I was taken aback by her appearance. Her face was grotesquely swollen, resembling a giant rubber balloon. Bandages obscured it, a stark reminder of the painful and invasive procedures she had undergone. At that moment, the weight of my emotions overwhelmed me. I felt every ounce of her suffering as if it were my own. But amidst the distress, I saw the fire of resilience burning within her. She was a fighter, determined to face whatever challenges came her way. Her unwavering faith in God provided her with strength throughout this arduous journey.

Reflecting on the earlier days of her hospitalization, I couldn't help but recall the neglect and shortcomings we had experienced. It had been nearly a week, and I noticed that her hospital gown remained unchanged, and she hadn't been given a proper bath. The stale odor permeated the air, a testament to the lack of attentive care. My wife confided in me that one night, she had desperately tried to call the nurse station due to a dying patient next to her. She pleaded to be moved to another room or even the hallway, consumed by fear. But her calls went unanswered throughout the night. Despite the presence of numerous staff members, her pleas were ignored.

It was a painful realization that the quality of care she deserved had been neglected. However, my wife's unwavering faith and determination remained unshaken amidst the frustration and disappointment. Her faith in God's guidance and protection gave her the strength to endure the physical pain and the emotional challenges that came her way. She refused to be defeated by the system's shortcomings, choosing instead to focus on her resilience and the unwavering support and love of our family.

This experience further reinforced the importance of advocating for oneself and actively participating in one's healthcare journey. We learned to speak up, assert our needs, and seek the care and attention my wife deserved. It was a difficult lesson that empowered us to navigate the healthcare system with a renewed sense of determination and assertiveness.

Together, we faced the obstacles that lay before us, relying on each other for support and finding solace in our unyielding faith. We knew that the journey would continue to test our strength, but we were resolved to overcome each challenge, one step at a time.

CHAPTER XXIII

· · · · ·

The Golden Rule

Determined to stand up for my wife's rights and well-being, I marched to the Nurse Station, ready to voice my complaints and concerns. I approached the nurse on duty, urging her to acknowledge the abandonment of care my wife had endured during her time at the hospital. However, it seemed as though my words fell on deaf ears. Frustration began to consume me, and I raised my voice, pounding my fist on the counter to make my point heard. I made it clear that if they couldn't provide the care my wife deserved, I would take her to Jacksonville, where her medical professional relatives resided.

At last, the nurse responded, explaining that there was nothing in my wife's chart to indicate that she required additional attention. It became evident that my primary care physician, Dr. Sam W., who happened to be the attending physician, had neglected my wife's needs. I couldn't help but feel that his actions stemmed from shame, possibly due to her lack of financial resources and insurance. The closure of our family business added to the difficult circumstances we faced.

Confronting Dr. Sam W. with the allegations, he vehemently denied any wrongdoing. Seeing someone I knew personally exhibit such a lack of compassion and understanding was disheartening. However, I realized I couldn't force him to change his behavior or acknowledge his actions. People's choices and intentions are ultimately their own, and all I could do was focus on my wife's well-being and the support of our loved ones.

At that moment, I recognized the stark reality that when financial resources and insurance are lacking in desperate need, some people may look down upon you instead of extending a helping hand. It was a painful realization, but it reinforced the importance of genuine friendships and the presence of those who stood by us during our darkest hours. It was a humbling reminder that circumstances could change, and those who once held positions of power or status may one day find themselves in need.

Time unfolded, and the power of God's workings became apparent. Ms. Thea R., the nursing supervisor at the station, who had acted with a sense of entitlement and neglect toward patients, eventually faced the consequences. Her department closed, she lost her job, and her colleagues dispersed. It served as a reminder that revenge is not in our hands but in the hands of a higher power. The concept of karma prevailed, teaching us that what goes around comes around. No one can hide from the consequences of their actions. It reinforced the importance of treating everyone with kindness and respect, regardless of their status in life.

Despite our challenges and disappointments, the unwavering love of God and the glimmer of hope kept us going. In the darkest of nights, hope always managed to shine through. We relied on our faith and found solace in knowing God would never abandon us. As we navigated this difficult journey, forgiveness became a crucial aspect. Although forgetting proved difficult, I embraced the notion of forgiving those who had caused us so much pain. As God had taught, loving our neighbors as ourselves was a challenging task, yet one we should strive for.

Taking matters into my own hands, I fired Dr. Sam W. as my wife's attending physician. We parted ways amicably, with a handshake and gratitude for the services he had provided. He asked if we could still be friends, and I assured him it wouldn't be an issue. It was a reminder that standing up for what we believe is proper garners respect, even from those in high-ranking organizational positions. I found new healthcare professionals for my wife, including an endocrinologist, neurologist, and primary care physician. Throughout this process, I was overwhelmed by the kindness and support we received from those around us.

The concept of what goes around comes around became even more evident in our lives. The good deeds we had done in the past came back to us through compassion and assistance from others. It was a testament to the power of positive actions and the interconnectedness of humanity. We learned that acts of kindness can return to us when we least expect it.

While forgiveness was something, I was prepared to offer, forgetting proved to be a more challenging task. The scars of the past were difficult to erase from our memory, but we understood that holding onto anger and resentment would only hinder our well-being. As we moved forward, we strived to embody the values of compassion, forgiveness, and love.

The experience with Dr. Sam W. was a stark reminder of the importance of the Hippocratic Oath that doctors take. Patient care should always come first, regardless of their financial situation. The focus should be on providing the best medical attention and support, putting the patient's well-being above all else. It was a lesson Dr. Sam W. seemed to have forgotten but would resonate with us for a lifetime.

Ultimately, our journey was not solely about seeking justice or revenge. It was about finding the strength to stand up for what was right, advocating for my wife's well-being, and relying on the support of those who genuinely cared. The road ahead was uncertain, but we faced it with hope, faith, and a belief in the goodness of humanity. We were ready to embrace the challenges, knowing that love and compassion would guide us through the darkest times.

Remember, there is always a flicker of light in every dark moment. And in every painful experience, there is an opportunity for growth, resilience, and a deeper understanding of the human spirit. Our story was beginning, and we were determined to make it one of strength, healing, and the triumph of love over adversity.

CHAPTER XXIV

· · · · ·

Surgery

As I sat in the guest waiting room, sipping my coffee, and nibbling on the doughnut, time seemed to stretch out endlessly. The minutes ticked by slowly, and each passing second felt like an eternity. The weight of anticipation and worry settled upon my shoulders, but I tried to remain hopeful and trust in the medical team's expertise.

To distract myself from the anxiety, I conversed with another guest in the waiting room. We shared stories, exchanged words of encouragement, and found solace in the presence of someone who understood the emotional rollercoaster we were both going through. The support of strangers facing similar challenges brought a sense of unity and strength at that moment.

As I glanced at the clock on the wall, I realized that several hours had passed since I left my wife in the capable hands of Dr. John P. and his team. My heart raced as I wondered how the surgery was progressing, hoping everything was going according to plan. I silently prayed for the success of the procedure and my wife's well-being.

Finally, after what felt like an eternity, a nurse entered the waiting room and called my name. My heart skipped a beat as I hurriedly followed her, eager to receive an update on my wife's condition. We walked down the sterile hospital corridors, our footsteps echoing with each step until we reached a small consultation room.

Dr. John P. stood waiting inside the room, wearing a tired but relieved smile. He explained the surgery, detailing the challenges they had encountered, and the measures taken to address them. Despite the difficulties, he assured me that the procedure had been successful, and they had removed the blood clot that threatened my wife's recovery.

Relief washed over me like a wave as I absorbed the good news. Gratitude welled within me, not only for the skill and dedication of Dr. John P. and his team but also for the unwavering support we had received from friends, family, and even strangers. The collective prayers and positive energy undoubtedly played a significant role in this outcome.

Though the journey was far from over, knowing that my wife had survived the surgery successfully filled me with renewed hope and strength. We still faced challenges, and the road to recovery would require patience and resilience. But at that moment, I felt an overwhelming sense of gratitude and an unwavering belief that we would overcome whatever lay ahead.

Leaving the consultation room, I returned to my wife's room, ready to embrace the next steps of her healing journey. We had faced obstacles and experienced moments of despair, but we were also reminded of the power of faith, the kindness of strangers, and the resilience of the human spirit.

As I approached her room, I whispered a silent prayer of thanks and prepared myself to be by her side, offering love, support, and unwavering belief in her strength. Together, we would navigate the challenges that awaited us, fortified by the knowledge that we were not alone in this battle.

· · · · ·

CHAPTER XXV

The Light at the End of the Tunnel

The doctor shared, "Good morning, Mr. De La Rosa! This is your wife's neurosurgeon speaking. I have prepared the reports for you, and I am pleased to inform you that yesterday's surgery went remarkably well. Given the size of the tumor, which was comparable to that of a golf ball, it presented challenges in maneuvering around the pituitary gland and hypothalamus. Due to the tumor's significant growth, the nostrils proved difficult to access. Consequently, I had to opt for the alternative route that I previously described to you. However, this procedure also impacted the optical nerve, making it an extremely delicate surgery."

"As a result, I regret to inform you that your wife will experience partial blindness or legal blindness. Her vision will be limited to a tunnel-like perspective. I am truly sorry to say that she will no longer be able to drive. Given the complexity of the surgery and her specific needs, your wife will need to remain in the hospital for several days, possibly even a month or more, to ensure she receives the necessary surgical care. The length of her stay will depend on her

progress and recovery."

"I understand that this news may be difficult to process, and it undoubtedly presents challenges for both your wife and your family. However, rest assured that our medical team will continue to provide the best possible care and support throughout her hospital stay and beyond. If you have any questions or concerns, please do not hesitate to reach out to me."

Oh! The hospital now feels like my second home. I often joke with my wife's neurosurgeon about how frequently I find myself there. Every day, I am by her side, caring for her, even while juggling the responsibility of getting our son to elementary school. As a family, we have made countless sacrifices for our loved ones. Through it all, we have realized that our God is truly incredible, faithfully looking after us.

The next day, the neurosurgeon returned with some news. "Mr. De La Rosa, I have something important to share with you today," he said solemnly. "We discovered a blood clot in the area where the surgery took place yesterday. It is imperative that we remove this clot immediately, which means we'll have to redo the entire surgical procedure." My heart sank, knowing how painful this would be for my wife. But Dr. John P. reassured me, saying, "Don't worry, Mr. De La Rosa. We will take care of it." I felt a sense of gratitude towards him for his dedication and expertise.

In moments like these, it's reassuring to have faith in the medical professionals and a higher power, knowing that they are working together to guide us through this challenging journey.

CHAPTER XXVI

· · · · ·

Answered Prayers

When I encountered the Nursing Supervisor, Ms. Thea R., that day, she startled me with her loud and aggressive tone. She began to question, "Who brought her here?" referring to my wife and the unique single bedroom designated for one patient. Ms. Thea R. further asked if I thought I could afford to pay for such accommodations. I responded, "Excuse me, Ms. Thea R., it was my wife's neurosurgeon who recommended her placement in this room. I suggest you discuss it with him." She stood there in stunned silence, seemingly at a loss for words.

Later, during dinner time, I was assisting in feeding my wife when, once again, the Nursing Supervisor approached and shouted at me, "Why are you feeding her? That will be your problem when you get home." At that moment, my frustration peaked, but I managed to control my temper. I realized that we needed more financial resources, employment, and insurance. We were entirely dependent on the benevolence of God and the hospital. Despite my overwhelming urge to shout back, I restrained myself due to our dire circumstances and lack of power. In times of helplessness and emptiness, only God can intervene on our behalf. So, that's what I did. With the omnipotent power of God, I conquered every obstacle. Evil may linger, but ultimately, goodness prevails. That's the essence of karma.

In the face of adversity, it is crucial to maintain faith and trust in a higher power. While the situation at the hospital was disheartening, I relied on the strength and guidance provided by God. Through His grace, I was resilient enough to endure and overcome these challenging circumstances.

CHAPTER XXVII

· · · · ·

No Man is An Island

When my wife was brought back to the ward after the second surgery, I was afraid at the sight of her swollen face. She appeared unrecognizable, and it was an uncomfortable moment for me. However, with the omnipotent power of God, in the following days, as the wrappings were removed, I gradually began to see my wife's familiar features again. I am immensely grateful to Dr. John P. and all the medical professionals who played a role in her successful operation. Without parting ways with our primary care doctor and seeking the expertise of Dr. John P., my wife's life would have been in grave danger. Now, she has a new attending physician, Dr. George Z., who is incredibly skilled and exhibits true professionalism, kindness, and compassion. He embodies the principles found in the Hippocratic Oath. Thank you, Dr. George Z.!

The healing journey my wife experienced was genuinely remarkable, primarily due to the incredible warmth and kindness of the people who surrounded her. Regardless of her financial status, she received the best possible care one could hope for. This experience taught me a valuable lesson: never underestimate or look down upon those who lack financial means or insurance. These external factors should never determine how we treat others. Everyone deserves equal respect and kindness. You never know when someone you may have overlooked or taken for granted will be the same person who extends a helping hand when you find yourself in need. Be kind to strangers. Be compassionate towards those in need. Be nice!

Forgiving and forgetting are not easy, especially when it involves individuals who have caused significant pain and suffering. This challenge is even more pronounced for impoverished people with nothing. It raises questions about humanity and the human connection. Why do such things happen? I've often heard the saying, "No man is an island." We cannot navigate this world alone without the support and assistance of the people we encounter. It is disheartening to witness the cruelty some individuals exhibit towards those who are poor and struggling to meet their basic needs. Instead of offering help, they prefer to let them suffer or perish out of shame. My wife experienced this firsthand during her time at the hospital. If I hadn't fought for her rights and advocated, she might have succumbed to her ailments prematurely. Eventually, karma caught up with those who had treated her with such disregard.

If you hold a job or consider yourself to be of high status, it is essential to remain humble. Do not look down on people; we are all God's children. We must love and support one another regardless of wealth or poverty. In the eyes of God, we are all equal.

CHAPTER XXVIII

· · · · ·

My Wife's Recovery

Finally, we are back home as a family—my wife, twelve-year-old son, and myself. My son had missed his mom tremendously during her extended stay at the hospital, and it had taken a toll on him, leading to a period of depression. However, I was grateful that the hospital provided us with various medical professionals to support my wife's recovery. We had a dedicated private certified nursing assistant and an RN who attended to her needs during specific hours of the day. The assistance we received went smoothly, and I decided to put work on hold until my wife fully recovered. By the grace of God, we managed to endure these challenging times with support from our relatives and, most notably, our friends in New Jersey. One individual who made an extraordinary impact on our lives was my wife's boss, Mr. Fargo P. His generosity and assistance were instrumental in helping us get back on our feet. He, indeed, was a wonderful person.

Above all, I want to express my deepest gratitude to my wife's Social Worker, Ms. Nieva M., who worked tirelessly within the hospital.

Ms. Nieva M. played a pivotal role in helping my wife navigate her financial obligations, including medical bills and doctors' fees. Through her efforts, we left the hospital with all our bills cleared. Ms. Nieva M., I cannot thank you enough. Without your assistance, we may have found ourselves burdened with overwhelming debts, facing the possibility of legal consequences, or struggling with monthly payments that could have lasted a lifetime.

These experiences have taught me that I am not alone in this world. I am no longer an isolated island. Just like a bird finally freed from a cage, to borrow from the poignant words of Maya Angelou's famous book, "I Know Why the Caged Bird Sings." We have been fortunate enough to receive the support, care, and love from the people around us. Their compassion and generosity have transformed our lives.

· · · · ·

Life Must Go On

It is truly disheartening when faced with difficult times, especially when those closest to us turn their backs. The closure of our store coincided with my wife falling seriously ill, and the responsibility of cleaning the ample space fell upon us. Despite reaching out for help, none of my relatives offered their support. It was a confusing and painful experience, leaving me to question the concept of love within a family. Did jealousy, envy, or something else leads them to abandon us? It's ironic because I had brought all of them to America, hoping to provide them with a better life—twenty-four family members. Yet, they were nowhere to be found when we needed them the most. Instead, our unknown neighbors extended their help, and within a mere three days, the place was cleared.

I proceeded to advertise and sell the equipment from our store, including walk-in refrigerators, freezers, coolers, display cases, and shelving. The response was swift, and all the groceries and equipment sold rapidly, bringing a sense of relief. This experience taught me a valuable lesson: never depend on others entirely. Rely on yourself and your own shadow. It is natural for individuals to seek the path of least resistance, often prioritizing their interests. This leads me to question the saying, "Blood is thicker than water." I am no longer sure about what has happened to me. Let us contemplate this particular case and be the judge. After all, I had brought twenty-four relatives to America, making numerous sacrifices along the way. Yet, in my golden years, they all turned their backs on me, significantly when my wife fell gravely ill and I was diagnosed with stomach cancer (non-Hodgkin's lymphoma) a year later. I underwent radiation and chemotherapy for three continuous months to eradicate the cancerous cells. Remarkably, the cancer is now in remission for over five years—an incredible miracle. However, I must continue to follow up with my oncologist for the next five years.

These challenging experiences have taught me that genuine support and loyalty may come from unexpected sources. It is a reminder to rely on oneself and maintain resilience in adversity. While family bonds are often considered vital, circumstances can expose their fragility. Yet, there is solace in finding strength within oneself and cherishing the kindness of those who offer help during difficult times.

CHAPTER XXX

. . . . .

God Helps Those in Need

As we returned to our old family convenience store, a new opportunity presented itself—a kind older man offered us the use of his expansive land nearby, approximately 20 acres, for farming or gardening. Intrigued by the prospect, I gathered my two brothers-in-law and two sisters to visit where the older man resided. We were welcomed by a picturesque scene—a charming cottage surrounded by fruit trees and other beautiful Florida perennials. This was their winter home, as they spent their summers up North. The vacant land lay in front of the cottage, with around a hundred cows peacefully grazing on the open field. Its proximity to the highway and the availability of electricity and water made it even more enticing. We were captivated by the offer.

The only task we were required to undertake was the care of the cottage's lawn, a skill one of my brothers-in-law possessed. With the agreement that we would receive free use of water and electricity, we gladly accepted the offer.

I recalled a customer of ours who owned a tractor, and I reached out to him, inquiring whether he could assist us with plowing an acre of land nearby for farming and gardening. Remarkably, he expressed his willingness to help us at no cost. It was indeed a miracle. Although we offered him some money, he refused to accept it, considering it a gift in return for the exceptional service we provided him when we had our store. We had cared for him during the good times, and now he was repaying the kindness.

Furthermore, we had a background in agriculture, which added to our confidence in this endeavor. After a week of land preparation, the soil was ready for planting. However, before we began, we needed to lay out an irrigation system for at least a quarter of an acre to ensure proper watering. Ordering all the necessary seeds online made the process even more convenient. Now, everything was in place for us to begin planting—a new chapter in our lives, cultivating the land, and reaping the rewards of our efforts.

CHAPTER XXXI

· · · · ·

Paco, Placido, Mia & Donna

It was a weekend when we began our planting endeavors. We had all the seedlings and seeds prepared for the task. Our planting sequence unfolded: Japanese eggplants, red and yellow bell peppers, Cayenne hot peppers, head-forming napa cabbage, climbing plants such as upo, squash, and finally, the yard-long beans. We managed to plant everything except for the yard-long beans, as we needed to construct a trellis for them to climb. Once that was done, we proceeded to activate the irrigation system.

I noticed that there was a little need for adjustment in the spacing between the pipes to avoid overlapping the sprinkler water, which led to excessive watering. I shared this observation with Placido and the other crew members. Placido was responsible for setting up the sprinkler system in the initial area. However, Placido appeared relatively reserved in response to my suggestion.

To my surprise, when we were supposed to work the following day, we waited for someone to show up. They didn't come back for the subsequent days either. They had turned their backs on me and abandoned the farm. The root of the problem lay in my brother-in-law, Placido, who had a superiority complex and believed he could not make mistakes. But does such a perfect person indeed exist? The reality is that no one is perfect, period.

Placido was pivotal in influencing my two sisters and my brother-in-law, Paulo. They chose to heed their advice instead of mine. I couldn't control their decisions, so I decided to carry on alone. My brother-in-law always sought to belittle me, but he couldn't succeed. He considered himself flawless, while in truth, he lacked humility. The notion of him being the perfect man in the universe was unfathomable.

I took care of the farm on my own while my brother-in-law, Placido, neglected his duty to mow the lawn. It was truly astonishing. This put me in a difficult position with the owner, who highly regarded me. I felt trapped in a precarious situation. It was profoundly saddening to question why my family would treat me this way. They seemed determined to bring me down, even though I had brought the entire family to America. It was disheartening to be treated as a person of no value. The pain I experienced was indescribable and unimaginable. How could I face the owner when he returned from the North and discovered the overgrown grass? I was filled with shame and had no courage to confront him directly. We didn't have any written contract because he trusted me implicitly as the principal caretaker. I was entirely at the owner's mercy, and I prayed to God for guidance.

When the owner returned in May, he summoned me to meet him at the farm. With the other three crew members nowhere in sight, I went alone. As I approached him, I could see the anger in his eyes, and he started hurling insults at me with the most offensive language possible. I felt like melting away right then and there. I immediately expressed my deepest apologies, taking full responsibility for everything. He commanded me to leave his property and clear whatever needed removal. I wanted to comply as quickly as possible. He didn't allow me to explain the circumstances that led to the situation. There was no mercy shown. All the blame fell solely on me. Later, I learned that the other two crew members had already faced their reckoning. They had passed away seven years ago. It was true what they say: what goes around comes around. The bad ones stay, while the good ones return to you.

So, Placido and his wife Mia (my sister) and Paulo and Donna (my sister) turned their backs on me. Placido was the instigator of this group's actions. How could they betray me like this? Is blood truly thicker than water? You be the judge! But God states that the evil deeds you commit will catch up to you, while the good ones will return to you. What goes around comes around. Vengeance belongs to the Lord. So, I chose to step back and believe that God would bring justice in front of me. This was not a prophecy, but it turned out to be true.

CHAPTER XXXII

......

A Disaster

Despite the immense pain and suffering inflicted upon me by my two brothers-in-law and sisters, I chose to forgive them. Forgiveness is both challenging and effortless. It requires great strength and the willingness to let go. Although the pain lingers and hurts deeply, I understand God commands forgiveness. I refuse to bear a burden that is not mine to carry. Instead, I surrender everything to the Lord, freeing my spirit from resentment. Revenge has no place in the hearts of humans. By offering everything to God, true liberation is attained. Why should I remain a prisoner of the past? It has vanished forever, and all that matters is the present moment. We must focus on today, for tomorrow is uncertain for anyone. I once asked God, "How many times should I forgive?" The Lord responded, "Seventy times seven." In other words, as many times as necessary.

Two days ago, I informed Paulo that we would work on the farm the following day at 10:00 AM, and he had agreed. However, it was almost noon when morning arrived, and he had yet to show up. When I reminded him, he became infuriated. He was gripping a machete tightly in his right hand and menacingly gestured for me to make the sign of the cross, which in his context meant a threat to my life. It was a terrifying moment, as we were in a remote location with no one around. Immediately, I turned to prayer. I pleaded with Paulo to stop and drop his machete, emphasizing that we are both children of God. Miraculously, he complied. We began to talk, and he listened. Amid this distressing situation, God swiftly answered my prayers, and I was saved. I am eternally grateful to our amazing God for His constant protection and grace.

CHAPTER XXXIII

· · · · ·

Black Sheep

During the mid-80s, I brought my black sheep brother, his wife, and their six children to America. They initially stayed in my house, but they moved out once they became established in their livelihoods. However, their departure turned my house into a chaotic place with twenty-four people. Constant fighting and noisy children made me feel ashamed in front of my neighbors. Whenever I tried to intervene, the parents would get angry with me. I was worried that my neighbors would eventually call the police. Thankfully, my neighbors showed kindness and understanding.

My black sheep brother only seemed interested in me when he needed something. Otherwise, he disregarded me and the rest of our siblings. When he set foot in America, he turned his back on us. Before his family's arrival, we were close companions. I did my best to support him and his family, but he never acknowledged it. He told everyone that they made it to America alone, disregarding all the affidavits of support documents I had provided. It hurt me deeply to realize he had been lying from the beginning. I couldn't even help my family without being rejected, let alone help our other relatives immigrate to America. I supported twenty-four of them. It's hard to comprehend the magnitude of that undertaking. Yet, they all resented me. I pray to God for forgiveness, as they do not understand the gravity of their actions.

When my black sheep brother needs something, he can act kind, but he has disowned me and the rest of our siblings. Our elder sister passed away just over three weeks ago, and he didn't even come to say goodbye. He never visited our other sick siblings and pretended they didn't exist. I cared for all our other siblings when they were ill until they returned to our Creator. What does it profit a man to gain the whole world but lose his soul? My brother and his family possess all the riches in the world, and I am not in competition with them. My life, along with my family, belongs to God. We do not possess anything in this world. Everything belongs to God, and He will be the judge. Unfortunately, my other siblings also treat me poorly. They turned their backs on me once they arrived in America and acquired wealth. I cannot comprehend what I have done to deserve such treatment. Despite not being wealthy, I have given them my all to help them. Once, I visited my younger brother, and as soon as I walked through the door, he screamed at me to leave his house. I left his house swiftly, feeling deeply hurt. My other sister did nothing to intervene. It felt like an unbearable emotional burden. My two elder sisters exhibit similar behavior to the rest of my siblings. They are not as highly educated as I am, and I believe their treatment stems from jealousy. I question why people want to hurt me and what I have done to provoke such reactions. I am a living martyr, prepared to be crucified on the cross.

I forgive those who have hurt me, as they are unaware of the actual consequences of their actions. Forgiveness is the highest and most beautiful expression of love. In return, it brings immeasurable peace and happiness. Resentment, on the other hand, is damaging and poisonous. It diminishes and devours the self, corroding like rust on steel until it is gone. Finally, I asked myself whether I should blame my mother for all the challenges in my life. I had initially considered becoming a religious priest, but I chose to obey my mother. Whether or not it was the right decision, I surrender everything to God, for He is the ultimate judge. Life must go on.

Despite my deep desire to pursue a life as a religious priest, I was at a crossroads when my family called upon me for help. Coming from a humble background, my mother and siblings relied on me for support, with my father already departed.

I had already begun my journey as a seminarian at St. John Catholic University, St. Benedictine Abbey in Minnesota. During my first semester, I received a letter from my mother urging me to quit my studies and return home. The responsibility and concern for my family's well-being weighed heavily on my heart, causing me great distress and turmoil.

My dream of becoming a monk and serving God had been a cherished secret since childhood. It was an aspiration I had held close to my heart, never sharing it with anyone. However, faced with the difficult decision, I sought solace and guidance from my faith and the divine presence.

Days turned into nights as I wrestled with my conflicting emotions. How could I divide myself between dedicating my life to God and fulfilling my duty toward my family? The answer, I realized, was not in separating my physical self but in recognizing that serving my family and serving God were intertwined.

In prayer and contemplation, I sought clarity and direction. I realized that by heeding my family's call and returning to their side, I would serve God through love, compassion, and support for those entrusted to my care. God's voice whispered in my heart, urging me to embrace my role in my family's life and be the helping hand they needed.

Although it was a difficult decision to abandon my path as a seminarian, I knew that my devotion to God and my commitment to His teachings would remain steadfast. Serving my family became my new mission, and I found solace and peace in surrendering to God's plan for me.

With a heart filled with gratitude, I thanked God for His guidance and accepted my role in the journey ahead. I knew I belonged to Him, dedicating myself to His service through the love and support I provided to my family.

Life's paths are not always straight and straightforward, but by trusting in God's wisdom, I found the strength to make the difficult choice and forge a new service course. As I moved forward, I carried with me the love and teachings instilled in me as a seminarian, incorporating them into my daily interactions and the care I bestowed upon my family.

My purpose may have shifted, but my devotion to God remained unwavering. In serving my family, I found a deeper understanding of God's love and presence in everyday moments of life. I knew that I was following the divine calling to love and serve others by embracing this new path.

And so, with renewed determination and a heart full of faith, I embarked on this new chapter, ready to fulfill my responsibilities to my family, guided by the teachings of my faith and the love of God.

CHAPTER XXXIV

· · · · ·

San Francisco

Indeed, life is filled with uncertainties, and we cannot change the past or predict the future. What matters most is the present, the choices we make today, and how we live our lives in service to others.

Reflecting on the path I chose to help my family, I acknowledge the challenges, pain, and suffering I experienced. Yet, I also recognize the profound fulfillment and gratitude that came from making a positive difference in their lives. My decision to prioritize my family's needs over my dream of becoming a religious priest was not without its difficulties. Still, it was guided by love and a sense of duty.

Had I pursued the path of priesthood, I could not know what might have unfolded in my life. It is a realm of possibilities and uncertainties. However, I can envision the potential hardships my family would have endured without my support. Growing up in poverty, with our parents already departed and with eight siblings, the chances of breaking free from the cycle of poverty would have been slimmer without my involvement.

The opportunity to pursue education and excel academically was a gift, and it bestowed upon me the potential to uplift my family from their circumstances. It would have been a disservice to my family, who needed me most, to avoid their cries for help. The love and care we all require as human beings should not be disregarded, especially within family bonds.

Looking back at the trials I faced, I find solace in the knowledge I contributed to improving my family's lives. Despite the pain and suffering, I am grateful for the chance to serve God by helping those closest to me. Our lives are intertwined with one another, and by extending a helping hand to our loved ones, we can make a significant impact on their well-being.

I am grateful to the Lord for guiding me through this journey, providing me with the strength and wisdom to make difficult decisions, and helping me fulfill my purpose in life. I take pride in knowing that I gave my best, sharing my thoughts, deeds, and everything good within me to create a happier world for those around me.

As imperfect beings, we will inevitably make mistakes along the way. However, by placing our trust in God and nurturing our faith, we can navigate life's challenges with greater ease. With God's guidance, things fall into place, and we can find peace and fulfillment in serving others and making a positive difference in their lives.

Ultimately, what truly matters is the love we share, the compassion we show, and the impact we have on the lives of those around us. By embracing the present moment and living a life of service and gratitude, we can find fulfillment and purpose in each day that unfolds before us.

CHAPTER XXXV

· · · · ·

Loving Enough, Forgiving Enough, And Forgetting Enough

When the golden years of my life arrived, I found myself plagued by illness, and no matter how many medications I tried, they provided no relief. I endured a challenging journey, navigating steep mountains, high and low hills, and treacherous, unpredictable seas (figurative speech). How did I manage to survive it all? Despite being an ordinary human being with the same emotions as others, I lacked the knowledge of loving, forgiving, and letting go of those who caused me pain throughout my life. Over the years, I suffered deeply at the hands of my family and others around me. The pain was immense, yet I couldn't release it; I carried it within me, burdened by the weight of the past, even though I shouldn't have. Then, earlier this year, I found myself in an ambulance, being rushed to the ER. However, I was turned away because I belonged somewhere else. I felt utterly lost. They transported me to an unfamiliar place where I couldn't bring anything. They provided me with new clothes and escorted me to an upper floor. The next day, a doctor examined me and prescribed several medications. Following the doctor's instructions, I was discharged. When I returned home, I carefully read through all the medical documents I was given. It revealed that I had been silently carrying Chronic Depression within me all these years—a condition that could have taken my life. My hatred towards those who hurt me weighed heavily on my heart. But now that I am aware of my diagnosis, I have decided: I will love those who have caused me pain; I will forgive those who have sought to harm me; and, most importantly, I will let go of the hurt inflicted upon me by others. In reality, these are the most difficult tasks to accomplish. Yet, God said: Love those who have hurt you; forgive those who have tried to destroy you; and, above all, let go of the pain caused by others. If I can genuinely embody these teachings, I will be rewarded with immeasurable peace and happiness throughout my life.

CHAPTER XXXVI

......

Looking Back

On the night of March 10, 2017, a dream unfolded before me—a vision that will forever remain etched in my memory. The scene was set in my ancestral house, nestled in the small town of Panganiban, the province of Catanduanes. As I slumbered peacefully within the walls of our family's wooden abode, a loud sound pierced the stillness of the night, capable of shaking our humble dwelling to its very core. The intensity of the noise resembled that of a colossal jumbo airliner descending on a bustling airport runway, resounding loudly enough to rouse even our faraway neighbors. And then, as abruptly as it had begun, the sound ceased.

In that instant, a towering figure materialized beside me on the bed. The faint glow in the room prevented me from fully discerning his countenance, but atop his head, I observed a crown of thorns with blood trickling down his face. Fear gripped me, compelling me to flee, yet my body seemed immobilized, ensnared by trepidation. Within seconds, as the aura surrounding him became unmistakable, I recognized his visage. Summoning my courage, I inquired, "Are you Jesus?" Doubt permeated my words, akin to the disbelief of doubting Thomas. He responded with a resolute affirmation. Still filled with uncertainty, I dared to pose another question, "May I see your hands?" And just like Thomas, he revealed them to me—each hand bearing a gaping wound, with crimson blood cascading forth. Emboldened by his presence, I asked, "Can I kiss you on your lips?" Regrettably, he declined. Intrigued, I questioned further, "Can we capture a picture to preserve the memory of our encounter?" Once again, his answer was a gentle refusal.

Following this exchange, he rose from the bed. He departed, descending the stairs with footsteps so weighty and resonant that their echoes reverberated throughout the house until they gradually faded away. A radiant figure emerged—a lady standing near a lamp, cradling a baby. She observed me with an unwavering gaze. Adorned in a flowing blue mantle that trailed down to her feet, she and the baby emitted an aura that bathed the room in luminosity. No artificial light source was needed to perceive their presence. The lady possessed a breathtaking beauty, her tender smile evoking a mirrored smile upon my face. Just as I began to acknowledge their divine presence, I stirred, and instantly, the lady and the baby vanished from sight.

Even before my dream reached its conclusion, an unwavering conviction took hold within me—I was sure that I had been visited by Jesus Christ, accompanied by the Virgin Mary and the infant Jesus. Overwhelmed with gratitude and blessedness, I cherished the profound encounter I had experienced within the depths of my slumber—a treasured encounter with Jesus, Mama Mary, and Baby Jesus. This remarkable vision graced my consciousness on a Saturday night, forever imprinting upon my soul.

In the early hours of that Sunday morning, I found myself in a state of distress. As I attempted to rise from my bed to use the bathroom, I discovered that I was drenched, my blanket and clothes saturated with moisture. Panic set in as I realized I was unable to move. Paralyzed and weighed down by a heavy burden of helplessness, I felt trapped in our home, now filled with memories of a once joyous past, yet haunted by the absence of my beloved wife, who had recently passed away.

Alone and devoid of strength, I longed to reach out for assistance. My sister resided just two blocks away, and I yearned to call her for help. However, my limbs remained unresponsive, rendering me immobile. I screamed out countless times, tears streaming down my face, but my cries fell on deaf ears, absorbed only by the unforgiving walls of my bedroom. Desperate, I turned to prayer, beseeching my merciful God to hear my plea. Yet, even as I wept and pleaded with the heavens, my prayers seemed unanswered. I contemplated the possibility that time may be running out for me as I languished in partial paralysis, unaware of the cause. Could it be internal bleeding or a cardiac arrest? Countless questions raced through my mind, and the fear of dying alone gripped my soul. I yearned for a priest to administer the last rites, anointing me with the sacrament of Extreme Unction—a solemn ritual for Catholics.

And then, unexpectedly, I regained mobility in my hands and feet. Summoning all my strength, I reached for the phone and dialed my sister's number. She arrived at my door in a matter of minutes, and I managed to crawl and unlock it for her. With urgency in my voice, I implored her to call 911. Soon enough, an ambulance arrived, and I was swiftly placed on a stretcher and transported to the nearest hospital's emergency room.

A battery of tests was conducted at the hospital, leaving me uncertain. Hours later, around 10:00 AM, my doctor approached me, wearing a smile and a glimmer of excitement in his eyes. He began to deliver the news; his words were enveloped in relief and hope. "Mr. De La Rosa, I have news for you. All the necessary tests have been completed, and I can tell you that you are one of the luckiest men alive. The results indicate that you have cancer, but there's no need to worry. It's a benign non-Hodgkin's lymphoma located in your stomach. The surgery required to remove it is not complicated, and I can perform it tomorrow. You will also need to undergo radiation and chemotherapy for a shorter duration." Overwhelmed with gratitude, I expressed my heartfelt appreciation to Dr. Chan for the good news and his compassionate care. Thanks be to God, I thought, my spirits soaring beyond measure.

In the following three months, I underwent six rounds of radiation therapy and six rounds of chemotherapy. I anticipated some minor side effects, such as hair loss and temporary weakness due to the impact of the treatment, but I was prepared to endure them. Throughout the process, I remained hopeful, focusing on the belief that I would complete the treatment before the end of summer in 2017.

As I diligently followed up with Dr. Chan for one, two, three, four, and five subsequent appointments, he could no longer detect any trace of cancer. I had entered a state of remission, celebrating five years of cancer-free. With fervent prayers, I held onto the hope that cancer would never return, bidding it farewell and consigning it to the ocean's depths, frozen and forever vanquished from my life.

My journey, battling cancer and emerging on the other side, left an indelible mark on my spirit. It instilled a profound sense of gratitude and a renewed appreciation for the fragility and preciousness of life. Each passing day became a testament to the strength and resilience of the human spirit, and I vowed to live each moment with purpose and gratitude.

This heartfelt message is intended for individuals who are currently battling or might be facing the challenges of cancer. Instead of succumbing to fear, I encourage you to summon your courage and harness all the inner strength you possess. Engaging in prayer and maintaining open conversations with your supportive friends is crucial. Prioritize a nourishing diet and actively participate in social interactions to uphold your overall well-being. Above all, nurture and fortify your faith, regardless of your circumstances or location, and trust that everything will fall into place harmoniously. Please know that you are constantly in my thoughts and prayers. May God bless you abundantly.

CHAPTER XXXVII

· · · · ·

The End is Near

As I near the completion of this final book I am writing, I humbly pray for guidance, Lord, to convey heartfelt thoughts to readers worldwide, my cherished friends and family, or anyone who happens to come across my words. My deepest desire is for their happiness and every good thing this world can offer to be bestowed upon them. Above all else, I wish them love.

Let me begin by acknowledging that our lives are composed of countless moments, each spent in myriad ways. Some moments are dedicated to seeking love, peace, harmony, and happiness, while others are simply about surviving from one day to the next. However, amidst this complexity, a profound truth is waiting to be discovered—that life, with all its sorrows and joys, is meant to be lived one day at a time.

Within this perspective, we can uncover the most wondrous and awe-inspiring revelation. Whether we reside in a grand castle, surrounded by servants and abundant wealth, or struggle to make a living in a modest dwelling, we possess the power within us to find deep satisfaction and embrace the true essence of life.

As we are well-aware, we can savor each moment and embrace the gift of each day bestowed upon us by the Lord. Every new day brings with it the opportunity for a fresh start, renewed hope, and aspirations that can lead us toward fulfilling our dreams. By approaching each day with a sense of newness, we can genuinely relish and live life to its fullest.

There may be occasions when we wake up in the morning and find things not unfolding as we had hoped. New challenges and unexpected changes may arise, demanding our unique response. During those moments filled with frustration and disappointment, we must remember that by shifting our perspective towards a more positive outlook, we can invite positive outcomes into our lives.

Let us now turn our attention to the concept of survivors. Survivors are individuals who have faced adversity head-on and emerged victorious. They have encountered seemingly insurmountable odds yet have found a way to reach their goals, refusing to let pain define them indefinitely. Like myself, I, too, am a survivor of three adversities, which I have shared throughout the pages of this book. Life, as we know it, can sometimes be mysterious. We may live peacefully and joyfully, only to be suddenly confronted with unforeseen challenges. Life, indeed, can be unfair at times. However, survivors face the future with purpose and conviction, believing that God and time are on their side. They trust that each endeavor will yield its rewards. Survivors possess the wisdom to make the most of life by living one day at a time.

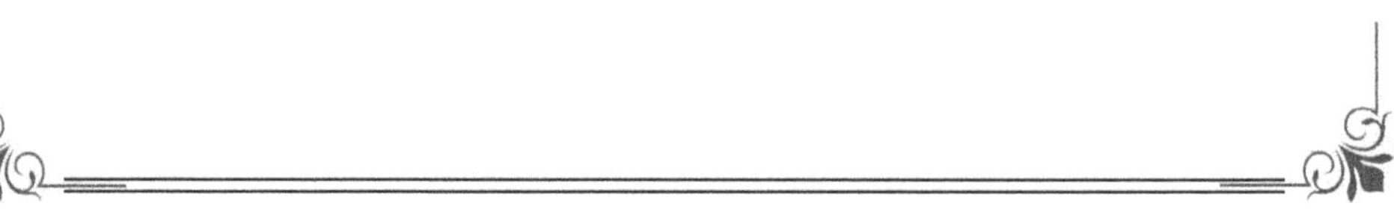

As imperfect human beings, it is crucial for us to recognize that we are not meant to be flawless. However, accepting this truth can be a challenging task. The best course of action we can take is to do our best and allow room for God to work in our lives. We cannot control every outcome in this world. Fortunately, we are fortunate enough to encounter individuals along our journey who are placed on our path to guide us, protect us, and touch our lives in their unique way. Through their presence, we can navigate life's challenges and emerge stronger.

Dear cherished readers, friends, and family, as I approach the completion of this book, I feel compelled to share with you my tender thoughts and warm wishes, hoping that they will brighten your day and keep a smile on your face – for your own sake and for all the souls you encounter.

May you always find serenity and tranquility in a world that may often seem beyond comprehension. May the inevitable aches and pains accompanying the passage of time grant you the strength to navigate through life, facing every situation with courage and optimism. Remember that there will always be those who love and understand you, even in moments of solitude. May you discover enough goodness in others to believe in a world of peace? Let kind words and warm smiles grace every day of your existence, both as a receiver and a giver. Teach your loved ones the power of love, and allow its embrace to accompany you as you venture into a world teeming with challenges. May the wisdom of those you genuinely admire become a part of you, a reservoir you can draw from whenever the need arises. Never forget that those whose lives you have touched, and those who have touched yours, will forever remain a part of you every day of your life. Embrace every precious moment that life presents to you.

Make it a point to find time each day to marvel at the beauty and wonders surrounding you. Recognize that every individual possesses boundless abilities, each unique in their way. Envision your future as one brimming with love, hope, and happiness. Learn to view every experience as valuable. Please gather enough strength to determine your worth, independent of the judgments of others. May you always feel loved and cherished.

The pleasures of life are there for you to embrace. Please share them with others, but always remember that you have earned the right to partake in them. Cherish those who love you, for they are a rare treasure in the journey of a lifetime. Return their love tenfold, allowing it to radiate from your heart and fill their lives, just as sunlight warms the Earth's darkest corners. Love is an endless journey, not a final destination; it traverses its daily paths. By doing so, your worries will dissipate like footprints in the sand. When anxieties and fears become your constant companions, take a moment to pause and listen. In silence, we hear the most profound truths. Listen attentively, and the gentle, caring words of encouragement from those who love you will permeate the stillness.

May these thoughts and wishes would accompany you on your journey, bringing comfort, joy, and a renewed sense of purpose. Remember, dear ones, you are cherished and cherished. You shall always be.

Embrace a vibrant enthusiasm for life. Choose to distance yourself from the worries and anxieties that accompany fretting. Live fully in the present rather than dwelling on the past or constantly worrying about the future. Seek out laughter for yourself and others and cultivate a spirit of joy. Take the time to appreciate the wonders of the natural world surrounding you.

Do not fear failure; instead, welcome it as an opportunity for growth. Lift your spirits and celebrate the gift of life. Above all, let us express gratitude to our compassionate and loving God who resides within each of us, reminding us that the impossible is indeed possible. Let us strive to embrace love, forgiveness, and the power of letting go.

Most importantly, let us thank God for reminding us that LOVE holds the key to all our questions, fears, doubts, and desires in our beautiful world of yesterday, today, and tomorrow. Life is a precious gift, so let us relish and enjoy it. Life is a melody, so let us sing it with all our hearts. Any moment is an opportune time for reflection, for letting go of differences, faults, and hurts, and surrendering them to God. May peace and joy accompany you in all your endeavors.

In conclusion, I would like to rephrase the poignant words of Oscar Hammerstein, the Broadway producer, to the beloved star Mary Martin before her performance in South Pacific. He wrote, "Dear Mary, a bell is not a bell until you ring it. A song is not a song until you sing it. Love in your heart is not meant to stay. Love is not love until you give it away." At the end of the performance, Mary

Martin, moved by Hammerstein's note, burst into tears, and shared, "Tonight, ladies and gentlemen, I gave my love away." I, too, am profoundly inspired by these words. Life is composed of countless songs, each with its significance and purpose. Listen to the music in your heart and let love resonate within you, filling your world and the entire world. When love permeates our lives, the whole world will sing along with us, united in love.

My dear friends, I implore you not to wait for others to extend forgiveness, for it is in forgiving that you become the master of your destiny, the Creator of a meaningful life, and the catalyst for miracles. Forgiveness is the highest and most exquisite expression of love. You will receive immeasurable peace and boundless happiness in exchange for your forgiveness. You will become the happiest person in the universe by loving, forgiving, and forgetting with abundance.

Reflecting upon my journey, I realize that I could have pursued wealth and fame, but only at the expense of the precious friendships I have cultivated. Now, as I stand at the threshold of life, I turn my gaze back to contemplate what I have accomplished with the years and days bestowed upon me, considering all that has transpired. I consciously chose to be known and cherished by a select few, and I would make the same choice if granted the opportunity to relive my life.

I have lived in the embrace of my family and friends, sharing in their joys and bearing witness to their sorrows, shedding tears alongside them. I have reaped a bountiful harvest from the fields of my existence. For me, this is more than satisfactory. I have lived to the fullest of my abilities, and I harbor no regrets for the time I have spent, even if it meant relinquishing the allure of material riches. When I look back, I consider myself to be the happiest person in the world. Mission accomplished! All for the Greater Glory of God.

About the Book

In my eighth book, I delve into the memoirs of my life, spanning from my roots in the Philippines to my experiences in the United States. Unlike my previous works that focused on the brighter side of life, this book delves into the challenges and struggles I faced. We all have stories to tell, including the difficult aspects of our journeys. Recognizing the importance of clearing the cobwebs from our minds and well-being, I share how this process is crucial in freeing our spirits from chronic depression.

Life's story is never flawless, as no one is perfect. Despite striving for perfection through constant repetition, events beyond our control can profoundly impact us. The fragility of life and vulnerability to various influences hinder our pursuit of perfection, as demonstrated in the example of marriage. My marriage ended disastrously, leaving me with three children. The separation was further complicated by family intervention and my children being taken away without my consent. This led me to endure silently, grappling with depression and PTSD. Amidst the pain caused by those who hurt and betrayed me, I found solace and strength in my faith in Our Lord Jesus Christ, choosing love, forgiveness, and the determination to move forward.

Starting anew in America presented its challenges, but I was driven by the belief in myself and the American Dream. Pursuing job opportunities with determination and enthusiasm, I secured a position as a Design Engineer in a construction company. My journey in America began successfully, and I felt proud and grateful for my new country, job, family, and neighbors.

However, life in the United States, the world's melting pot, exposed me to encounters with people from diverse backgrounds. Amidst pursuing the American dream, I faced both good and bad experiences. The world can be cruel, and I experienced this firsthand when my wife fell seriously ill, and we lacked the necessary resources for proper care. This harsh reality brought me closer to my family as I sought to uplift them from poverty in the Philippines. Yet, despite my efforts to help, I discovered the importance of love, forgiveness, and letting go of the past as I strive to become a better person.

In "The Power of Loving, Forgiving & Forgetting," I share my experiences with honesty and vulnerability, reflecting on the challenges and triumphs that shaped my life's trajectory. It is a story of overcoming adversity, finding strength in faith, and embracing hope for a brighter future.